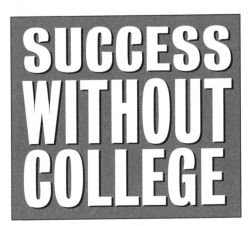

SUCCESS WITHOUT COLLEGE

Careers in Art and Graphic Design

Ronald A. Reis

BARRON'S

All inquiries should be addressed to:
Barron's Educational Series, Inc.
250 Wireless Boulevard
Hauppauge, NY 11788
http://www.barronseduc.com

International Standard Book No. 0-7641-1629-0

Library of Congress Catalog Card No. 00-046779

Library of Congress Cataloging-in-Publication Data

Reis, Ronald A.
    Careers in art and graphic design / Ronald A. Reis.
        p.   cm.—(Success without college series)
    Includes index.
    ISBN 0-7641-1629-0
    1. Commercial art—Vocational guidance—United States.
    2. Graphic arts—Vocational guidance—United States.   I. Title.
        II. Success without college.
    NC1001.6 .R44 2001
    741.6'023'73—dc21

                                                                00-046779

Printed in Hong Kong
9 8 7 6 5 4 3 2 1

Table of Contents

Acknowledgments   v
Overview   vi

CHAPTER 1

Beyond the Starving Artist   1

Art Everywhere   3
Fine Art Versus Commercial Art   3
Reality Check   4
Specialized Training   6
Training for the Art-Techno World   6
Jobs Austin's Parents Never Heard Of   7
Art-Techno Opportunities   8
A Dozen Ways to Go   9
Companies That Are Doing It   11
People Who Are Doing It   12
A Few Key Points to Remember   15

CHAPTER 2

Point and Click   17

The Computer as a Design Tool   18
Getting People "Right"   19
The 3-D Touch   20
Waiting for WYSIWYG   20
Blame It on the Mouse   21
Techno Animations   22
Mastering the Electronic Paintbrush   24
Point, Click, Go   25
Companies That Are Doing It   26
People Who Are Doing It   28
A Few Key Points to Remember   31

CHAPTER 3

Education and Training   33

The DPD Institute   33
Not Your Typical Student   34
A B.A. Is Not the Only Way   35
Theory and Practice   35

What Industry Wants   36
No More Party, Party, Party   38
A Grand Academy   40
Extreme Signage   42
Ready to Join the CIA?   43
Advertise It Loud and Clear   44
Creativity, That's What It Is All About   44
Asking the Right Questions   45
Schools That Are Doing It   46
A Few Key Points to Remember   49

CHAPTER 4

Artists and Illustrators   51

What Is a Graphic Artist/Graphic
   Designer?   52
Animation and Game Design: Not All
   Playtime   53
Fashion Illustration: Drawing the Draped
   Body   55
Signage Everywhere: Art by the Yard   57
Book Illustration: Beyond the Written
   Word   59
Illustration: A Diverse Field   61
Companies That Are Doing It   62
People Who Are Doing It   63
A Few Key Points to Remember   69

CHAPTER 5

Graphic Designers   71

Web Mania   72
A Photo Opportunity   75
A Package Deal   78
Multimedia, Multiple Skills   80
The Digital Divide   83
Companies That Are Doing It   83
People Who Are Doing It   84
A Few Key Points to Remember   89

CHAPTER 6

Product Designers 91

Jewelry Design: Art in Miniature 92
Toy Story 94
Exhibit Designers 97
Interior Designer 100
Taking Shape in Three Dimensions
   102
Companies That Are Doing It 102
People Who Are Doing It 104
A Few Key Points to Remember 109

CHAPTER 7

Interning in the Arts 111

Interning: All but Required 112
A Fifty-Fifty Proposition 114
Avoiding the Interning No-No's 114
The Co-op Option 116
The Résumé: Door Opener 117
Portfolio: Talent Indicator 118
Information Interview: See and Be
   Seen 120
Out and About: Attending Industry
   Conferences 121
People Who Are Doing It 124
A Few Key Points to Remember 127

CHAPTER 8

The Company Artist 129

In House 130
Design Firms 132
Advertising Agencies 135
Which Way to Go? 137
Bringing Home the Dough 138
Companies That Are Doing It 139
People Who Are Doing It 141
A Few Key Points to Remember 145

CHAPTER 9

Freelancing 147

To the Rescue 148
As Good as Your Last Job 149
Hustle, Hustle, Hustle 150
With a Little Help from My Rep 151
A Competitive Environment 152
Going for It 153
Companies That Are Doing It 154
People Who Are Doing It 155
A Few Key Points to Remember 159

Resources 161

Index 165

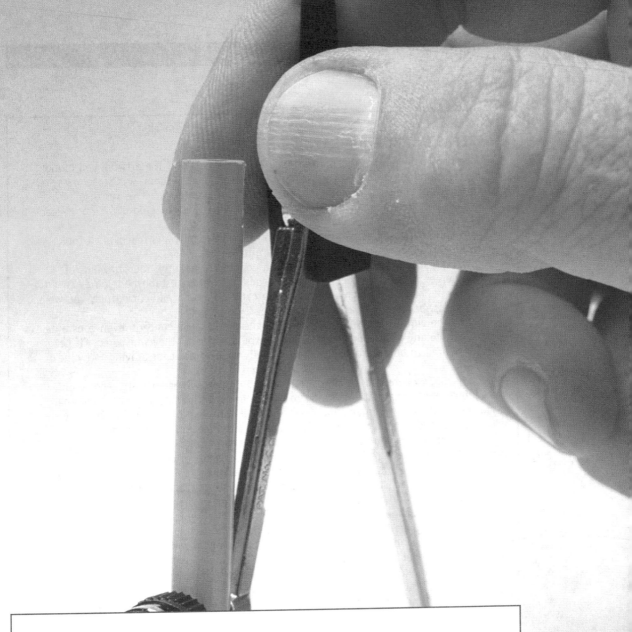

Acknowledgments

The writing of this book required input from numerous individuals, associations, educational institutions, and firms doing art and graphic design. I wish to thank all those who contributed their time, suggestions, and materials. Many of you are quoted in the book. And to those who are not, rest assured your voice has been heard. Particularly, I wish to thank Sharon Tate, Dean, Service Careers, at Los Angeles Trade Technical College, for her input on the book's organization. I am also indebted to Max Reed, Senior Editor at Barron's, for shepherding the project through to completion, always being available to answer questions, and providing encouragement and support.

Ronald A. Reis

CAREERS IN ART AND GRAPHIC DESIGN

Perhaps it began in kindergarten, or even nursery school. The artwork you brought home, to be hung proudly by your parents on the refrigerator door, was somehow different. Your use of color, form, shape, proportion, even perspective set the drawings, sketches, and colorings apart—beyond what was expected of a 5- or 6-year-old.

As you progressed through grade school, friends, family, and teachers all took notice. You had, they were sure, a talent, a gift, for art.

In high school you took art classes and doodled constantly. Your drawings of action heroes, souped-up cars, and your friends' pets firmly established you as an artist in the making. Though you had yet to earn a dime for all your output, you were, nonetheless, becoming an artist in everyone's eyes.

And therein lies the rub. Along with all the praise came concern, even consternation, particularly from your parents. "What, would happen," they whispered, "if he really wanted to be an artist, somehow actually tried to do it for a living? Why, he'd starve!"

So, that's where you are now. What do you do next? Does your art become only an interesting avocation, something to dabble in as you pursue a "real" career—law, medicine, computer programming—one that will earn you a good living? Or can you, contrary to the popular misconception, actually make decent money as an artist?

This book says you can. Commercial artists and graphic designers get paid for what they do—they don't work for free or trade services for eggs or chickens. As advertising illustrators, animators, book jacket designers, calligraphers, comic book creators, display artists, fashion illustrators, interior designers, jewelry designers, logo designers, model makers, multimedia designers, set designers, sign painters, technical illustrators, toy designers, photographers, forensic artists, and web page designers, artists and graphic designers are making a living.

Furthermore, in many fields a college degree is not required. Money is to be made in the commercial art world by those who possess talent, skill, a great portfolio, and, yes, education and training in the arts beyond high school. *Careers in Art and Graphic Design* shows you what to expect and how to get there.

There are nine chapters in this book. Chapter One debunks the "starving artist myth," while exploring the world of working artists and graphic designers. Chapter Two introduces the greatest revolution in commercial art and graphic design since the paintbrush—the computer. Chapter Three explores the training and education you will need to succeed in what all agree is a competitive, supply-exceeds-demand field.

Chapters Four, Five, and Six deal in depth with a dozen careers. As examples of what artists and graphic designers can do without a college degree, we look at the animator/computer game designer, fashion illustrator, sign graphic artist, and book illustrator. We examine the careers of a web page designer, commercial photographer, package designer, and multimedia designer. And we explore what it means to be a jewelry designer, toy designer, display artist/exhibit designer, and interior designer.

Interning, for those studying art or graphic design, is a must. In Chapter Seven we see what interning and related activities, such as interviewing and visiting trade shows, are all about and how you can gain maximum benefit from them. Because most starting out in art and graphic design will find jobs working for someone else, we examine in Chapter Eight what it's like to work in house, for a design studio, or for an advertising agency. And in Chapter Nine we explore what it means to go out on your own, as a freelancer, an entrepreneur.

Throughout, each chapter includes a listing and brief description of companies in the field and, except for Chapter Three, profiles of individuals doing the work. Resources dealing with professional organizations and publications are also included. What others recognized early in you as a gift can become a satisfying, lifelong career. Welcome to careers in art and graphic design.

CHAPTER ONE

Beyond the Starving Artist

G raphic Designer needed immediately, 1 yr exp min. Must be able to meet deadlines. Must have experience with HTML, Photoshop, Java, 3D/2D. Flash, Shockwave, Active X preferred. Excellent wage & benefits.

Graphic Artist. Exp in gen'l magazine layout, knldg. of Quark Exprs. and Photoshop. Illus. a plus. ABC Enterprises.

Artist/Graphic Production. Mac Artist. Heavy workflow, tight deadlines. MUST know Photoshop/Illus/Quark.

Graphic Artist. Selected candidate will design & produce all graphics for web sites, print advertising, branch and corporate promotion materials; assist in research for design and navigation of web sites.

Are there jobs for artists and graphic designers? As the above ads from a major newspaper indicate, there are indeed. And, furthermore, in many cases you don't need a college degree to get one. You do have to be educated in art and design principles, and you must know how to use the

latest drawing and layout tool—the computer. With both, you can be on your way to an exciting career in art and graphic design.

Austin felt it was time to have a serious talk with his parents. After all, he would be graduating from Monroe High School in two weeks, and, let's face it, they had a right to know what he was planning.

So, with Mom and Dad sitting across from him on the couch, Austin begins:

"It has been in me for some time," he says, fidgeting with his favorite paintbrush. "I need your understanding and your support. I've got to be free to pursue my inner voice, my purpose, my vision. Mom and Dad, I have decided—I want to be, I am going to be—an artist."

Frozen in their cushions, Mom and Dad remain momentarily speechless.

"What will our friends say," Mom eventually declares, hand to mouth.

"You can't do that," demands Dad. "You will never get a job. You'll starve!"

"Of course, your drawings are excellent," Mom interjects. "Haven't we always told you so? But, we didn't mean to, well, encourage you, at least not to this extent."

"You are so good with computers," brightens Dad, "why not a career in programming?"

"Actually, I will be using my computer skills a lot in art and design," says Austin. "The computer is a required artist's tool now."

"What about business," Mom probes. "You were always interested in helping your father down at the store. Business school is where you belong."

"I'll have opportunities galore to use any business skills I acquire," Austin explains. "I may eventually freelance or actually open my own design shop."

"You're great with people, son," enthuses Dad. "Maybe a psychologist, or even a psychiatrist?"

"Doing art and design in the commercial world is a collaborative team effort," Austin responds. "Getting along with fellow workers, suppressing my ego, will be a psychological challenge."

"But wouldn't you have to move to New York or Los Angeles to get a job?" Mom questions. "How can you expect to find work as an artist here in St. Louis?"

"Artists and designers are needed all over, Mom," says Austin. "And with the digital revolution, particularly the Internet, I can do work anywhere and send the results everywhere," he added.

"It's going to be all right, Mom, Dad," Austin finally states, wanting to wind up the conversation. "I'll attend the local community college; they have a great two-year A.A. degree program in art and graphic design. And I can continue to live right here at home with you. We'll all save a bundle! I'm telling you, it's an artist's life for me."

ART EVERYWHERE

If you're either just starting out, graduating from high school or switching careers in midlife, convincing family and friends, schoolmates, and coworkers that an artist's life is for you will be a challenge. The starving artist image is so widespread, so ingrained, that sympathy, accompanied by a quizzical look questioning your sanity, is what you'll get from nearly everyone you confide your secret ambition to.

Sure, the paintings of van Gogh, Rembrandt, and Gauguin are now worth millions—but didn't these famous artists live in poverty? As the saying goes, "As an artist, you'll have to die before you can make any money."

Art and design, particularly graphic design, is all around us. We see it in greeting cards, magazines, book illustrations, clip-art catalogs, on gift products, posters, prints, record labels, T-shirts, mugs, toys, cans, and boxes, to mention only the obvious.

Then there's animation and computer games, cartoons and comic strips. And every web page on the Internet needs art—who better to create it than artists and graphic designers?

Artists also work as costumers, fabric designers, pop-out art creators, in signage for movie theaters, and even as tattoo designers. Yes, art is everywhere. And its creators don't do it for free. They are paid for their services.

FINE ART VERSUS COMMERCIAL ART

Professional artists and graphic designers are known as commercial as opposed to fine artists. Yet, when "artist" is mentioned, it is the latter that most people picture.

Unfortunately, fine artists find it tough earning a living. Such folks often work at other jobs to support their art; commercial artists prepare for a career in which their talent will support them.

The difference between a fine artist and a commercial artist is that the former works to satisfy his soul. He can make a painting blue if he wants to, just because he wakes up blue in the morning. The commercial artist, on the other hand, must solve someone else's problem, and in doing so, must make money.

Perhaps James Bratek, an art director/graphic designer in West Orange, New Jersey, sums it up best: "The main difference between the two is that commercial art is client-driven. In contrast, fine art is self-driven in that the artist creates art first and looks for buyers second. Commercial art and fine art both have their respective supporters and detractors, but neither side should cancel out the other."

REALITY CHECK

No one says it's going to be easy making money for yourself or someone else in commercial art. Competition is keen in all but a few specialties. And be advised: As a commercial artist or graphic designer, you'll enter a profession where supply always exceeds demand.

"It's considered a glamorous field," says Victor Aello, of the UCLA Professional Designation Program in Graphic Design. "And today, with the new technology, everyone thinks he or she is an artist or designer."

"The toughest part of my job," says Bert Johnson, a graphic artist at *Graphics Two*, "is the lack of knowledge, even appreciation, in the customer base. You work on a project for days, then the client announces, 'My cousin Fred says we should do it this way.' You want to scream. Graphic artists must understand they're not fine artists. We work to satisfy someone else's need, not our own."

But that's okay, you say. As long as there is work to be done. There is, but you will have to compete for it.

To better appreciate and understand the role of art and graphic design in your own life and the resulting career prospects, pick up that CD sitting next to your stereo. Now consider this, according to Jana Gary, of the Printing Industries of America (PIA):

- An art director put together the initial concept for the insert and the cover.

- A writer wrote the text copy.

- A photographer snapped the necessary photos.

- A technician scanned in the photographs.

- A graphic designer generated the image on a computer.

- A page layout artist streamed in the copy.

- A prepress technician prepared the film and plates for the printing press.

- A press operator printed the insert.

- A binder folded the insert down and put it in the case.

Notice that nine people, none of whom even (necessarily) play a musical instrument, were involved in the process of packaging your CD—nine job categories in just one small aspect of the graphic arts industry.

Clearly, in an age of convenience and throwaway packaging, artists and graphic designers can expect to keep busy producing an ever-increasing number of books, catalogs, boxes, magazines, labels, food packages, directories, financial and legal documents, business forms, brochures, newspapers, and greeting cards.

Okay, so the jobs are there. Great! But what do they pay?

Well, according to U.S. Department of Labor data, commercial artists and graphic designers, of which there were approximately 230,000 nationwide in 1998, had average annual starting salaries of $26,000. With experience, that salary can go up to $50,000, or more, a year. Yet, in certain specialities, such as computer game design, the numbers are truly alluring. One study reports that most salaries are between $70,000 and $90,000 a year. And starting salaries range from $45,000 to $55,000 a year. Not bad! (For more complete salary data, see Chapter Eight.)

SPECIALIZED TRAINING

To get these jobs and command these salaries, however, you need specialized training.

"The definition of commercial art has changed dramatically in recent years," says Susan North, of a Twin Cities design college. "Commercial art can include multimedia, illustration, graphic design, 3-D, and computer-generated graphics. But all require some pretty specific training. It is quite competitive, as all arts-related occupations tend to be, but there are new companies popping up all the time."

Let's face it, graphic arts is one of the professions that has been completely transformed by computers. Designers now do their work with sophisticated software. Computer proficiency is really key; people have to know Quark and Photoshop. It is practically impossible to get a position in graphic design today without knowing these programs well.

TRAINING FOR THE ART-TECHNO WORLD

According to a spokesperson at Platt College, an institution in Cerritos, California offering a diploma and associate degree in art and design, the graphic design world is an increasingly technical world. Art and analytical skills are merging.

The Platt program illustrates what type of education and training are needed to succeed in this new art-techno world.

Built on three levels, one begins with foundation courses in the fundamentals of graphic design.

Next, computer graphics courses are taken, where design skills are enhanced using advanced computer technology for layout, typography, illustration, and electronic prepress problem solving.

And third, interactive multimedia is studied, combining sound effects, video, animation, and film to produce unique designs.

Welcome to art and graphic design in the new millennium.

JOBS AUSTIN'S PARENTS NEVER HEARD OF

The concern Austin's parents have about his pursuing a career in art or graphic design would, perhaps, be lessened if they knew what opportunities await him. Graphic design is one of the fastest-growing professional fields in the world. According to the 2000–2001 *Occupational Outlook Handbook*:

> Employment of visual artists is expected to grow faster than the average for all occupations through the year 2006. Demand for graphic artists should remain strong as producers of information, goods, and services put increasing emphasis on visual appeal to produce design, advertising, marketing, and television. The explosive growth of the Internet is expected to provide many additional opportunities for graphic artists.

There's that magic word—Internet. But why should we be surprised? The Internet and World Wide Web have changed everything.

Here are just a few jobs in art and graphic design that probably didn't even exist ten years ago, all based on digital technology. Austin's parents, listen up!

- 2-D and 3-D animation

- Computer game design

- Electronic illustration

- Internet communications

- Digital photography

- CD-ROM game design

- On-line magazines

- Web page design

ART-TECHNO OPPORTUNITIES

Bill Allen, editor/publisher of *3D Artist*, a glossy bimonthly magazine in Santa Fe, New Mexico covering the computer graphics scene, knows about art-techno possibilities.

According to Allen, opportunities, to a certain extent, are where you make them. Lawyers who need work done for presentations in the courtroom and architects who don't have the time to learn the skills necessary to do architectural walk-throughs are turning to 3-D artists. Often the principals wind up battling with dueling animations.

In the CD-ROM world, where duels appear on screen, opportunities are exploding—all across the country. As one developer explained, "A CD-ROM game I am familiar with was developed by a six-person team, the members of which met for the first time when it was over. If you know the software: Lightwave, 3-D Studio Max, and the like, you're on your way. Yet, you must have a vision. It is not enough to be technically good; you need to be an artist first."

Indeed. All this talk about technology is fine and necessary, and in Chapter Two we look at technology, particularly the computer, in depth. Yet, at the core is the artist, the creative visionary. According to the American Institute of Graphic Arts (AIGA), all graphic designers share three common traits: interest in the *visual* world, *curiosity* about communication in all its forms, and *creativity*. The organization sums it up this way:

> The accelerating communications advances urged onward by the invention of movable type, papermaking, printing, the Industrial Revolution and urbanization, as well as the recent explosion in both print and electronic mass media, have put design and designers in the important and influential role of cultural mediators. They work in the intersection between commerce and art, between industry and the public.

Increasingly, graphic designers are called upon to mediate among visual, verbal, and numerical information, and, indeed, to create meaning out of mere data, communications out of information.

A DOZEN WAYS TO GO

While there are, literally, dozens of careers in art and graphic design that we might explore in some depth, we will, in this book, examine 12 in particular. We chose these 12 for three reasons. One, they are interesting career specialties; many require the use of the latest technology. Two, these careers span the spectrum in the art and graphic design world. And three, none demand a college degree, at least not for entry-level work.

The dozen careers we explore can in turn be divided into three groups, each consisting of four careers. In group one, covered in Chapter Four, we investigate careers of artists and illustrators. In group two, Chapter Five, we examine careers that graphic designers engage in. And, in group three, Chapter Six, we look at the work of product designers.

Let's preview a few of these careers, ones we'll be examining later, in more detail, in Chapters Four, Five, and Six.

- **Animator/Computer Game Designer.** Though a good-looking guy, it isn't vanity that keeps Colm Duggan staring into a six-inch mirror, perched above his animation disc. Doing so is a job requirement. As an animator for Rich Animation Studios, Colm must keep "making faces" in order to draw them. We meet Colm and explore the career of animator in Chapter Four.

  For Stevie Case, a computer game designer at Ion Storm, doing game design is a natural. Having been a game fanatic all her life, Stevie finds that designing games is a perfect career for her. We'll find out about this ideal career in Chapter Four as well.

- **Web Site Designer.** Steve Buchsbaum, president and CEO of Creative Edge Enterprises, Inc., a web site design firm, started out in the film industry, eventually working on such projects as *Star Trek: The Next*

Generation, *Quantum Leap*, and *The Quest*. Now he uses his postproduction skills to design award-winning web sites for organizations such as the Los Angeles Dodgers. We probe the ever-exploding career of web site designer in Chapter Five.

- **Commercial Photographer.** Kathryn Russell loves food. She also enjoys taking pictures. The combination has made her an accomplished food photographer whose clients include Nestlé, Target, Disney, and Ralph's Market. But even after 15 years in the business, she still must show her work and prove her pictures are better than the next person's. We'll see what being a commercial photographer, particularly in the digital age, is about in Chapter Five.

- **Toy Designer.** Toy designer Gabriel Delatorre chose toy design as a career because, as he says, "Where else can you get a job assignment to design a really cool toy and then play with the results all day?" Of course, toy design is not all fun and games, as we'll see in Chapter Six. Still, it's a great place to use your arts-and-craft skills to, as Gabriel says, "Sketch today what some kid could be tossing around on the playground tomorrow."

- **Interior Designer.** It's far more than picking out the right draperies and bed coverings. Knowing computer-aided design (CAD) is critical, for example. Being able to design on a computer is essential. But keep in mind, CAD is not an alternative to traditional design methods but a necessary complement.

So as we've seen, plenty of opportunities await Austin as he seeks to live his life as an artist. With dedication, focus, and discipline, he will succeed. His parents should be excited and proud, and eager to encourage his dream.

COMPANIES THAT ARE DOING IT

Not surprisingly, art and graphic design companies are advertising on the Internet, broadcasting to the world what they have to offer. Here are a few examples.

3-D Maker
http://www.3dmaker.com/
Specializes in 3-D art and animation, video, and postproduction effects for the Internet. Features an on-line gallery and links to client sites.

Admedia
http://www.ad-media.com/
Provides services encompassing advertising, marketing, design, and web development. Explores product examples in the portfolio.

Amplifier Creative
http://www.ampart.com/
Kansas City company that focuses mainly on print and web design. Offers an extensive on-line portfolio, as well as contact information.

AV Design/Media Maker
http://www.advmm.com/
Salt Lake City multimedia production studio that offers video, audio, editing, and graphics design. Offers a list of equipment and services.

Baggs Studio
http://www.baggstudio.com/
Provides business graphics in the shape of illustrations and embroidery. Includes a list of clients, an art archive, and telephone numbers.

Colorgraphic Signs
http://www.colorgraphic.com/
Designs and produces event signs and tower signs for retailers, shopping centers, and trade show exhibitors. Browse service and pricing available.

People Who Are Doing It

MEET SHERRY SCHLOSSBERG

VITAL STATISTICS

Sherry, forty-two, is from Cherry Hill, New Jersey. One day, not many years after graduating from high school, she saw her mother addressing bar mitzvah invitations. Sherry asked to help. When she discovered people got paid for scrolling beautiful letters on envelopes, stationery, and the like, Sherry got excited. With a baby in diapers and the need to work from her home, she had found a career. Sherry, now living in California, has been lettering ever since.

❏ PRESENT JOB

Sherry freelances, doing calligraphy for artists, graphic designers, and often Hollywood's elite.

❏ LOVING THE WORD

"When I started," Sherry says, "there were no schools, no classes, and few books to inspire or help the novice. Today, there are workshops and seminars galore."

Sherry can earn $100 for doing a single word, though she often has to do that word over and over again to get it just right. "That word," she says, "which might wind up as a logo on a box of crackers, on corporate stationery, or in a major ad campaign, has to be perfect."

❏ PAYING THE BILLS

Most calligraphers (including Sherry) most of the time do not earn anywhere near $100 a word. "It's often envelopes, certificates, and stationery, the drudge work of the profession," she says. "Every calligrapher has to do it. No one likes it; it's repetitive, boring, not terribly creative. But it does pay the bills."

MEET JEAN HILL

VITAL STATISTICS

Jean, twenty-seven, lives in San Antonio, Texas. After earning her associate degree in commercial art from Golden West Community College in 1994, she went to work for Sunset Magazine *photographing beautiful gardens. Then, three years ago, Jean built a custom studio behind her garage. When she's not on site, she is holed up there, shooting photos.*

❏ PRESENT JOB

Freelance photographer specializing in photographing metal racing rims for clients such as American Racing, TSW, Epic, GNC, and Beckman.

❏ HEAVY METAL PHOTOGRAPHER

"I've become well known for shooting bright, shiny metal," Jean says. "Clients bring high-intensity, polished wheels to my studio. I end up creating the glossy images they need for brochure and magazine layouts."

For freelancers like Jean, finding and keeping clients is crucial. "In this profession, acquiring clients who consistently bring you business is key," she says. "Yet, it's a game. You don't always know where the business will come from. I can be busy for three months, then for a month have no work at all."

❑ KEEPING THE WORK COMING IN

Jean knows how competitive commercial photography can be, but she's undaunted. "If you are good, you'll work," she says. "You must be technically skilled and know how to use your equipment well. In addition, it's necessary to be a problem solver and able to exercise a good idea. Make your clients look terrific through the pictures you take. If you remember that simple point, you're going to work."

MEET STEPHANIE OCCHIPINTI

VITAL STATISTICS

Stephanie is a jewelry designer who graduated with an associate degree in jewelry design from the well-known Fashion Institute of Technology (FIT) in New York City. It was at FIT that she really learned about jewelry, how it is constructed from beginning to end, whether it is cheaply made. She learned you can't just draw a pretty picture of a piece and call it design. "Can it be made?" is always the bottom-line question.

❑ ELEMENTAL FORM

For Stephanie, being able to condense a concept into its elemental form is what jewelry design is all about. "There are a lot of designs out there that are full of frippery. They don't make sense. A line of jewelry needs to have a cohesive feel. When it does, you'll know it. It's like with writers—you can tell one from the other by their vocabulary. No one would mistake Hemingway and Faulkner."

❏ PERSONAL HIGH

It has not always been easy for Stephanie; her jewelry career did not take off until she began winning national awards. Today, however, she is in demand and turning down work all the time. "Having control over your career is what it's all about," she says. "Yes, a paycheck is great; the money is nice. But finally being recognized in your field is a personal high."

A FEW KEY POINTS TO REMEMBER

- Artists and graphic designers are needed everywhere.
- Commercial artists do it for a living.
- Competition for jobs is keen.
- Employment of visual artists is expected to grow faster than the average for all occupations through the year 2006.
- Skill with graphic design software is crucial.
- The digital revolution has expanded opportunities for artists and graphic designers.
- Web page design is a key growth area for graphic artists.
- Graphic designers must mediate among visual, verbal, and numerical information.
- In many cases, a college degree is not required, but postsecondary education and training is.

CHAPTER TWO

Point and Click

According to *Animation Magazine,* computer animation, including the motion capture variety, will continue to account for an increasing share of the production pie. With such independent CGI (computer-generated image) houses as Pixar, PDI, Blue Sky, and Mainframe hooking up with Disney, Dreamworks, Fox, and IMAX, look for alliances with the likes of Rhythm & Hues and Digital Domain, which long to switch from special effects to doing their own fully animated films. On the TV side, the lure of low-cost motion capture technology will help accelerate a shift toward computer animation of all kinds.

And what about web animation? Such animation will prove increasingly important for independent studios that have been adversely affected by the recent consolidations in the entertainment industry. While some web animations will undoubtedly morph into regular TV shows and feature films, they will increasingly become part of a distinct and independent segment of the animation industry, as well as a surefire replacement for video demo reels.

THE COMPUTER AS A DESIGN TOOL

And that's just "A" for animation. No matter what aspect of art and graphic design you're into, the computer as a design tool is making an impact.

Interior designers use software programs such as AutoCAD and Form-Z to render objects in three-dimensional space, applying lighting, texture mapping, and camera angle modification.

Being able to design on a computer is essential. Not as an alternative to traditional design methods, but as a necessary complement.

As with all image-producing endeavors today, digital technology is also transforming commercial photography.

"The digital camera, which results in the ability to store and manipulate a filmless image, is revolutionizing our profession," says James Lewis, a photography instructor at a two-year community college. "Though the capital investment is still high—$25,000 for a first-class setup—soon all professional photographers will go digital."

If you're into packaging, printing, advertising, and other graphic communications, the ability to use digital design tools is key. Today's designers use a word-processing program to type text documents, *Adobe Illustrator* to create logos and illustrations, and *Adobe Photoshop* to scan, enhance, and manipulate photos. Then they take these individual elements and import them into *QuarkXPress* to design and produce a final page layout with image and text boxes, basic typography, style sheets, and columns.

Let's face it, to advance as a graphic designer/visual communicator, you must know how to use these tools. You have no choice; knowledge and skill with the Big Three is required.

And of course, by definition, web page designers design on the computer. Now the fastest-growing medium on earth, the Web, for designers, didn't even exist in the early 1990s.

With its interactivity that includes text, graphics, animation, sound, and movies, the Web offers a brand-new working world for artists and graphic designers. Using programs such as Dreamweaver to edit, and Flash to create vector-based animation graphics, web page designers push the envelope in the fastest-growing segment of the design industry.

And fortunately for designers, the Web is an ever-changing medium.

"When I first started designing on the Web, I had to totally change my attitude about the work," says Sabine Messner, of *Hotwired*. "I was used to print, where I would get this moment of relief when I had the final product in my hands. But on the Web you're never done."

GETTING PEOPLE "RIGHT"

This from a recent review of Adobe's LightWave 3-D:

Raytracing, motion blur, MetaMation, inverse kinematics (IK), Bones, field rendering, lens flares, compositing—they're all here. With LightWave 3-D's OpenGL and QuickDraw 3-D, you can see your creations in real time. Available on Windows 98, Windows NT, Power Macintosh, DEC Alpha, Silicon Graphics, Inc., and Sun Microsystems.

Who understands this stuff? Computer science nerds, maybe, but artists and graphic designers? Yes, if they want to succeed in today's commercial art and graphics world.

Janet Smith of Admedia knows what's going on. One after another, she makes it her mission to conquer the latest design software.

Her most recent triumph? Poser 4.0, a Metacreations release. With Poser, Janet can create images or animations that involve human figures and animals. She chooses figures from a library and then poses them. Next, Janet customizes their look by applying colors and textures. She can set the figures or parts of them in motion using what is called keyframing. Then Janet renders either a still image or an animation sequence.

Poser can do all this because it understands inverse kinematics, the ability to link and limit positions that limbs can be put in.

How? When you select the hips of a figure and move them, Poser will move the legs accordingly so that the feet stay in position. But if you grab a foot and move it, the hip and other leg stay in place.

Getting people right has always been a problem in animation. Accurately positioning figures or parts of their bodies is the challenge. With Poser, you have a handle on the problem (though it takes practice), even if you are familiar with other 3-D programs: 3-D Studio Max and Form-Z, for example. Without that knowledge, it will take a lot longer.

THE 3-D TOUCH

Speaking of 3-D, modelers have long worked in clay to create three-dimensional images. John Neil, founder of Prop and Custom Incorporated, is one such artist.

"I got started sculpting Christmas ornaments for Hallmark in Kansas," he says. "Today, it's latex machine guns for *Universal Soldiers 2*, a baby dino for *The Lost World*, and a 'Doctor Evil' console used in the *Austin Powers—The Spy Who Shagged Me* film."

But as with most commercial artists, the digital world is intruding on John's modeling environment, too.

"I saw software at a trade show recently that blew me away," he says. "The program allows you to sculpt in 'clay,' using a computer-enhanced tool. Holding the stylus, you can feel the material's resistance. I need to get that package."

John may have to wait a bit for the chance. Sure, the software he craves, FreeForm from SensAble Technologies of Cambridge, Massachusetts is available, but it costs $15,000.

Still, FreeForm is an amazing advance, with the potential to revolutionize modeling for users in applications such as toy manufacturing, industrial design, and entertainment. But like all software, this program isn't learned in a day. Even if John could afford FreeForm, it would take him some time to feel comfortable using it.

WAITING FOR WYSIWYG

Artists and graphic designers did not take quickly to the World Wide Web. As a design opportunity, it was seen initially as having limited possibilities. Born of the Internet in 1991, the Web began as a text-only tool for disseminating information. In 1993, with the creation of Mosaic, the first browser able to display graphics, that changed.

At last, information on the Internet could have color and personality. All of a sudden, the Internet became more than a way to exchange useful information and e-mail; it became an entertainment medium.

Still, designers were not drawn to the Web en masse. After all, there was that HTML stuff. Did designers have to be programmers?

Known as Hypertext Markup Language, HTML is a set of tags developed by early web creators to mark a text document's structural elements. Until recently, it has kept artists and graphic designers away in droves. Not anymore. With today's WYSIWYG (what-you-see-is-what-you-get) web design programs, such as Macromedia's Dreamweaver, Microsoft's FrontPage, GoLive's CyberStudio, and Adobe's PageMill, you can design pages without writing a single line of HTML code. Though seen by some code-savvy web builders as a crutch for rookies, the latest WYSIWYG HTML editors are a godsend for professional designers.

While computer programmers are still needed in the web development world, artists and designers, thanks to WYSIWYG, are assuming the leading role.

David Taylor, a longtime web page designer at Intuitive Systems, puts it this way: "Programmers compete with quality off-the-shelf solutions. If you have a knack for programming, great! But many more web page designers than web-savvy programmers exist. With large design teams, the ratio is ten to one—ten times as many content providers, graphic designers, and managers than programmers."

Ron Azim is one such designer. Working in Dreamweaver 3.0, on a PowerPC with 64MB of RAM, a 19-inch, high-resolution monitor, and the Mac OS 7.5.5 operating system, Ron feels like the pro web designer he is.

"Dreamweaver's interface takes a little getting used to," he says. "The screen tends to get littered with floating tool palettes and file windows. Still, with some careful placement and pruning, I can make it easier to use."

WYSIWYG aside, remember: Good design is still what it's all about.

BLAME IT ON THE MOUSE

Patented in 1970 by Douglas Engelbart and originally referred to as the X-Y Position Indicator, the hand-wielding mouse attached to your computer is today almost as ubiquitous as its namesake; there are probably half a billion tethered to PCs and Macs around the world.

Apple Computer gets credit for coming up with the first commercially viable version. The computing world has never been the same. Though some artists complain about its unnatural feel, as a graphics input device it definitely beats the keyboard. And it's here to stay.

Like the safety pin, the humble mouse has withstood the test of time. As designer Barry Katz puts it, "It is cheap enough, small enough, and good enough, and should be counted as one of the significant success stories of twentieth-century design."

Of course, without software, computer hardware (mouse included) is useless. Together, they have had a profound impact. There is no question about it—computer technology has altered forever the way artists and graphic designers think, create, and work.

Of course, digital art has its critics. Often, such art is dismissed because, it is said, there are too many layers between the artist and the final product. It supposedly somehow lacks the human touch of "real" art. Some figure the software did all the work.

But addressing that issue and a unique aspect of digital art—its endless reproducibility—Bruce MacLeod says, "Anyone creating art of any kind that can be endlessly duplicated runs the risk of being dismissed regardless of the tools used to create it. This duplication factor is a much more compelling threat to the credibility of digital art than a measurement of the creative input at the software front end."

TECHNO ANIMATIONS

John Judy, a graphic designer specializing in CD-ROM development for Oracle, got started in design because he saw all the T-squares, triangles, Rapidograph pens, and drawings boards, and figured the tools didn't change much.

"That was the late 1980s," he says. "Boy was I wrong."

Indeed! But watch out! The latest technology can be enticing—too much so, perhaps.

"There is tremendous seduction there," says Adam Watkins, a graphic designer at Utah State University. "I fell into the trap myself, always looking for the next great tool, program, application. But I wasn't creating anything substantive."

Students today are well-trained in the latest technology, but are they receiving an equally solid grounding in conceptualization or traditional design tools like line, form, color, and typography? Take animation. If a person does not understand the esthetics and the design, the resulting animations seem like techno animations rather than artistic animations. Such students can tap into all the gizmos, plug-ins, and special effects programs, but their animations wind up being ugly.

The bottom line: A Mac alone does not a designer make. Technology is not a substitute for design expertise. Let's face it, designing with a computer probably demands more artistic talent than creating with a pencil and paper.

Just as having a pen or word processor does not make me a better writer, technology will not help designers be better visual communicators. Remember, a computer can't draw for you. You must come to it with some sort of artistic background, innate or through training.

"You need both, the artistic talent and the technical skills," says Sharon McCall, a design student. "You look at a TV commercial where someone lands atop the Empire State Building and an artist will know if it looks realistic. Someone just using the program with no art background won't have a clue. To get toward realism, you must merge the two—art and technology."

Clearly, there are three kinds of artists out there. About 50 percent know the technical side. Another 30 percent, the creatives, don't know how to turn a computer on, and maybe 20 percent know both. The latter are the highest paid and tend to do the stuff they really like to do. That's the combination everyone is looking for.

It is what Pixar relied on when they created *Toy Story 2*. Commenting on the cost of producing the sequel, Galyn Susman, supervising technical director, says, "The software isn't what's expensive; it's the talent. We definitely improved our tools over the orginal, but it is the sensibilities of our artists that have made the sequel so much richer and more textured."

Art and technology—the combination is explosive. A firm grounding in art and graphic design fundamentals coupled with skill in the appropriate software gives you a winning combination. But how to get started with the technical? Computers can seem so intimidating.

MASTERING THE ELECTRONIC PAINTBRUSH

"I've always seen them as big electronic toys," says Elaina Fleming, a Flash-based animator at Flinch Studios. "You know, an electronic paintbrush." She's lucky. Not all who come to computers from art and graphic design are so in love with—and confident of mastering—the new tool. As one student explains, "It was a tremendous struggle for me. At first it was sheer panic. But I was determined. In the beginning I was in a complete fog, but little by little the veil lifted."

Keep in mind, while the learning curve is steep, you don't have to master everything at once. Many programs will take years to learn well.

For some, learning a computer application means taking a course. For others, reading a good book on the subject and following its tutorials will get them started. And there are those who just like to play around, see how things develop. That's the approach Josh Jeffe took.

His software experience had actually been in the music industry. Josh worked for a couple of companies designing MIDI synthesizers and samplers. Then, while looking for something new to do at the time, he bought a Mac II and one of the first 32-bit video cards that became available for it, and just started messing with graphics in his spare time.

Regardless of the approach you take in learning about computers and gaining the skills necessary to produce quality work with your chosen application, remember these points:

- If after sitting in front of a computer, even for only ten minutes, you get up knowing more than when you took your seat, that's progress.

- You're learning an application, not how to program.

- You don't have to master the application all at once. In fact, you'll probably never know all there is to know about Flash, Director, LightWave, Ray Dream, Maya, 3-D Studio Max, or even Illustrator, Photoshop, and QuarkXPress. What's more, you don't need to.

- Most software is almost foolproof with regard to any damage you can do. The worst that might happen is a loss of data if you fail to save your work properly.

- A great way to learn is to hire a mentor or tutor. For $20 an hour, you can probably get a student to spend time showing you, one on one, whatever it is you need to know. For $200 you would get ten hours of individualized attention. That should place you way up on any learning curve.

POINT, CLICK, GO

All computers are not the same—but almost. Actually, there are two main platforms: Mac and PC. Which one should you choose?

It doesn't matter. While there are those in both camps who will challenge you to a duel in defense of their chosen platform, in reality almost all the applications you might want to master are available for use on both Macs and Windows-based PCs.

However—and this is important—the graphics world, from prepress to production, has for years been dominated by Macs from Apple Computer. Exchanging files with those who work in art and graphic design will be easier if you are Mac-based, no doubt about it.

So if you are just starting out and can afford it, the Mac may be your best choice. But either way, Mac or PC, the main thing is to get going. That's what Austin is doing. Not waiting until he graduates from high school, he is taking a night course at the local community college while still a senior. "It's a short introduction to Illustrator, Photoshop, and QuarkXPress," he says. "I love it."

A recent survey in *How Magazine* revealed that for two out of three creatives, keeping up with technology is a top priority. So borrow a computer, rent one, or take the plunge and buy one. Then begin by tackling one of the Big Three or an equivalent: Adobe Illustrator for illustrations, Adobe Photoshop for image editing, and QuarkXPress for page layouts. The excitement is just beginning. With that said, J.D. Jarvis, writing in *EFX Art & Design*, gets the last word:

> Digital is not here to put an end to anything. Rather it is here to expand all things, to combine and to make more things attainable. For the artist, it is the edgiest work of all, the biggest, most exciting challenge in a long history of the synthesis between technology and hand and mind and heart.

COMPANIES THAT ARE DOING IT

Here are more examples of graphic design companies that are advertising their services on the Internet.

AD Cook and Associates

http://www.adcook.com/
Services include stylized and realistic digital illustration, logo development, brochures, and web design. View a portfolio and a client list.

Artworks Graphic Design

http://www.artworksdesign.com/
St. Louis firm that specializes in logo design, web page creation, company literature, and marketing materials. View sample work and contact details.

Brackett-Zimmermann Associates

http://www.brackett-zimmermann.com/
Offers watercolor, pencil, gouache, pen-and-ink, and computer illustrations. Scan illustration styles, a portfolio, and a client list.

CLIK Productions

http://www.clikproductions.com/
Washington, D.C., company that combines graphic design, illustration, and web art. View a portfolio of work, or link to client web sites.

Creative Media Development
http://www.creative-media.com/
Offers integrated creative development and production of graphic design, multimedia, film, video, training, meetings, and events. Also offers a portfolio.

Custom 3-D Graphics
http://custom3d.turbocom.net/
Web site design company that offers samples of logos, banners, client sites, and image maps. Learn about banner advertising and scanning images.

People
Who Are Doing It

MEET MARTIN PHELAN

VITAL STATISTICS

Martin Phelan, thirty-two, lives in Montreal, Canada. After earning his night school diploma in graphic arts, he worked as a technical writer for two years. Looking for something a bit more creative and artistic, he began teaching desktop publishing. From there it was on to animation, learning from the artists around him.

❏ PRESENT JOB

Martin is Product Evangelist for Crater Software, makers of CTP (Cartoon Television Program) software that creates realistic cartoon-style animations using CAA (computer-aided animation). "It acquires images an artist has drawn, scans them in, colors them, assembles them over a background, and adds movement," Martin says. "The result is what you see on the Saturday morning series."

❏ DOING THE BUSY WORK

"Traditional 2-D cel animators who like to draw with a pencil have been slow to adopt computer-aided animation techniques," Martin continues. "They have been a bit wary of the new technology. But with CTP, they have a modern tool with a simple, easy-to-use interface. What once took studios with thousands of employees many labor-intensive person hours to complete can now be done in one-tenth the time. It's far more productive.

"In the old days, each drawing would have to be traced onto celluloid, physically painted, and a picture taken of each frame. When you consider there are 24 frames per second, a two-hour feature animation results in 172,800 pictures. A lot of work!"

❏ YOU'RE HAPPIEST DOING WHAT YOU'RE HAPPY DOING

As Product Evangelist, Martin travels North America showing tractional animators how to use CTP. "I tell them it allows image capture from virtually any source, whether it is video, scanner, or standard image files," he says. "Line-testing, inking and painting, camera movements, and video input can all be performed within a single-window interface. It's as simple as using a pencil."

Martin loves what he's doing. "You're happiest doing what you are happy doing," he says. "I am proof of that. I work within the creative process, with creative people. I enjoy interpreting between engineers who design software and the artists who use it. I am always challenged mentally and artistically."

MEET MARK FAVERMANN

VITAL STATISTICS

Mark Favermann, fifty-two, lives in Boston, Massachusetts. He is the founder of Favermann Design. Established in 1978, the studio does environmental and graphics design, specializing in branding, identity, way finding, and signage programs. The firm was one of five to be selected to comprise "The Look of the Games" for the 1996 Atlanta Summer Olympics.

❏ ELECTRONIC ETCHASKETCH

"It's only a tool," Mark says, echoing the familiar refrain about computers in the design world. "Whether you're doing animation, computer arts, digital imaging, graphic design, multimedia, special effects, video games, web site design, or 2-D and 3-D modeling, the computer is not something greater than the sum of its parts. Many people who devote themselves to computers see them as having anthropomorphic features that are simply not there."

Today, Favermann Design employs six creatives, though that number nearly tripled during the Olympic project. "When we began that assignment, we computerized, too," Mark says. "It took us only two weeks to be up and running. That tells me it's not all that mysterious a process."

"No doubt about it, though, computers have made it more efficient for us," he continues. "We don't need as many people drawing things, cutting and pasting."

❏ TRENDS AND FADS

Mark believes technology is having a significant and positive impact on how designers work and what they do, but he does raise cautions. "A while back, you saw lots of animations on the Web," he says. "I may be wrong, but I don't see so many anymore. It was a technique, a fad, a teachable skill that someone without a design sense could do. And the results showed.

"We are at a crossroads now," Mark advises. "When the printing presses came in, they displaced illuminating manuscript monks, but the books the monks worked on were beautiful. I don't yet see a parallel in the computer world. Look at *Wired Magazine*; it's practically unreadable. Yet someday the look will be there. I'll keep looking."

A FEW KEY POINTS TO REMEMBER

- Being able to design on a computer is essential.
- The World Wide Web is the fastest-growing segment of the design industry.
- It can take years to learn some software applications well.
- With WYSIWYG it is possible to design web pages without writing a single line of HTML code, though knowledge of HTML is quite helpful.
- WYSIWYG aside, good design is still what's important.
- Computer technology has altered forever the way artists and graphic designers think, create, and work.
- Watch out! The technology can be seductive, perhaps too much so.
- You must come to the computer with some sort of artistic background, innate or through training.
- You don't have to master an application all at once.
- Two out of three creatives say that keeping up with the technology is their top issue.

CHAPTER THREE

Education and Training

After years of neglect, the arts are on the mend in many American public schools. One reason, of course, is that the strong economy is filling state coffers, making it possible to restore music and arts specialists. Researchers are also finding that engaging students' creativity enhances their performance in reading, speaking, listening, and math.

THE DPD INSTITUTE

In summer, when the temperature reaches 100°F plus, they swelter. In winter it's cold, the structure's steel framing adding its own chill. Still, they come, from as far away as Fresno, to this 150- × 20-foot self-storage metal bunker in Thousand Oaks, California, a town 40 miles north of downtown Los Angeles.

It is here that Sheldon Borenstein, a longtime Hollywood animator, demonstrates drawing techniques at the "Borenstein Art School in a Box," or, officially, the DPD Institute. The focus is on classical training; no computer animation courses are offered. Yet 300 students have signed up for 12-week classes covering head and hand drawing, as well as animation skills. The cost? From $250 to $300 per class.

Attending art school "in a can" may seem strange indeed. But that's the lengths to which some will go to make it in the commercial art and graphic design world. As student Johanna Spinks says, "You know, you have to struggle for your art. So when it's freezing in the morning, or in the summer when it's hot as hell, I think of all the people who have struggled before me."

NOT YOUR TYPICAL STUDENT

Opportunities to acquire art and graphic design education and training exist all over, at all levels. From afternoon Regional Occupation Programs (ROPs) for high school juniors and seniors in California to prestigious art institutes offering advanced degrees across the country, art studies are available to nearly anyone.

Cheryl Williford isn't just anyone, although she's not your typical art or graphic design student, either.

"I was a poor single mother working two or three jobs at a time—waitressing, tending bar, delivering flyers," she says. "Then, one day, I noticed animation software on my brother's computer at his office. I was fascinated."

Using software and tutorial books from her brother, Cheryl began poring over the material every night. She began to get the knack of it.

Cheryl continued to teach herself animation and eventually started taking classes. Then when a college near Cheryl's home launched a certificate program in multimedia, she borrowed money to pay for the class and even took a leave of absence from her day job to do the course.

Today, Cheryl is an Internet developer for MCI WorldCom.

This single mother's route into animation and web development is not the path for everyone. Still, what Cheryl did illustrates the commitment needed to enter such demanding fields. It shows also that it is possible to gain entry-level work in art and graphic design without a four-year degree.

Sure, a bachelor's degree is always desirable, but today, an associate degree or a certificate program can also work. In some cases, these shorter programs—two years for an associate degree, as few as six months for a certificate—are better for jump-starting your career because they offer specialized, focused skill training. Later on, once you're working, you can pursue a B.A. part time.

A B.A. IS NOT THE ONLY WAY

That B.A., no doubt about it, is the traditional entrance into art and graphic design.

And why not! An undergraduate (four-year) degree from such highly acclaimed schools as the Art Center College of Design in Pasadena, California to the New England School of Art and Design in Boston, Massachusetts or hundreds of colleges and universities in between, represents a considerable achievement. Those who are able to gain entrance, have the time to devote to a four-year course of study, and can afford to attend, are likely to get an excellent education in the fundamentals of art and graphic design, as well as training in the latest tools of the trade.

But the bachelor's degree is not the only way in—far from it. With more than 1,300 postsecondary, nondegree (B.A.) institutions (public and private) nationwide offering some form of education and training in the visual arts—short-term courses and certificates or the two-year associate degree—you needn't wait four or five years to get started as an artist or graphic designer.

If time is critical, cost a factor, or you're just busting to get to doing animation, designing computer games, or creating multimedia CD-ROMs, such programs are worth exploring.

"I just want to start working as soon as possible," says Jose Hernandez, a twenty-year-old student majoring in graphic design at his local community college. "I need to earn a living. I haven't written off getting my B.A. degree. It'll just have to come later."

THEORY AND PRACTICE

Choosing a college or art institute, even one at the two-year level, can be tricky. We'll look later at specific factors to consider. For now, it's best to remember that to have any chance of succeeding in a field where you'll be competing with many four-year college graduates, you must be both educated and trained in the arts.

- Education encompasses the history, the theory, the principles, the fundamentals of the discipline. It's about learning, thinking, understanding, and preparing for a lifetime of growth and change.

- Training involves acquiring specific skills and the ability to perform a given task, whether it is traditional fashion illustration or modeling with 3-D Studio Max.

- Education without skills won't get you a job. Training without an education will prevent you from launching that job toward a career.

Author Mark Oldach, in his excellent book, *Creativity for Graphic Designers*, sums up the need for both when referring to the computer and its role in design:

> The computer is both blessing and curse rolled into one expensive tool . . . It is the pencil of the late twentieth century, nothing more . . . Too many designers use it as their only tool or, worse, as a substitute for thinking. These designers use the computer as a sketching tool, thinking tool, writing tool, typesetting and illustrating tool . . . Then the tool has mastered the designer, not the other way around, and the designer may have begun abdicating his responsibility to the computer. Theory and practice—the right combination at any level of study.

WHAT INDUSTRY WANTS

Before choosing a course of study, it would be wise to look at what industry expects from art program graduates. Here are the recommendations of a labor market analysis done for the interactive digital media industry. The six points listed apply just as well to any art and graphic design discipline anywhere in the country.

- Virtually every company interviewed stressed the importance of having a solid foundation in the techniques and theory underlying the skills used to create interactive digital media products. Even though software tools are constantly changing, the underlying theoretical elements remain constant.

- Industry also emphasized that schools should incorporate project-based learning involving teams throughout their curriculum to develop the following core competencies: Problem solving, creativity, teamwork, knowledge of the production process, understanding of interactivity, and communications.

- Since jobs are often temporary, freelance, and project-based, industry recommended that schools prepare students for self-managed, flexible careers. Schools should provide classes in basic business and entrepreneurial skills.

- Bringing real-world experience into the classroom was also stressed by industry. A class such as Production 101 would provide the opportunity to experience the nonlinear process involved in the production of an interactive digital media product. Students would also learn the roles of the various team members and how their individual contribution fits into the whole team effort.

- Because portfolios rather than résumés are used by industry to evaluate job candidates, classes should be provided that advise students on how to prepare and professionally present their work.

- Employees who have a strong foundation in the theory of interactive digital media are able to adapt to technology and market changes. Lifelong learning is an essential element of a career in this industry where software tools are constantly changing. Employees who are wedded to a particular tool set will soon find their careers dying as new tools emerge.

There's plenty to contemplate when selecting your education and training program, and a career in art and graphic design.

NO MORE PARTY, PARTY, PARTY

"Don't look a gift horse in the mouth."

"Birds of a feather flock together."

"Don't put all your eggs in one basket."

"You have to crawl before you walk."

"Too many cooks spoil the broth."

Common phrases, all. Could you, using just type, illustrate any one, expressing the phrase in line, shape, color, and value? That's what instructor David Opheim's first-term graphic design class at Platt College in Cerritos, California is doing. Using traditional tools—pencils, markers, templates, T-squares, triangles, and cut-and-paste materials—students employ knowledge of type and basic design criteria with a strong dose of creativity, to achieve balance and contrast in a lively image.

"Don't put all your eggs in one basket" is Larry Hyde's choice. A nontraditional student for sure, Larry has a degree in business from the University of Southern California. After working in finance for a dozen years, earning a six-figure income, he decided to act on his high school counselor's advice.

"She told me I would be sorry some day if I didn't do what I really wanted to do," he says. "She was right. I figured with my general education requirements already out of the way, I can complete the A.A. program here at Platt in as little as 11 months. As long as the stock market doesn't dive, I can afford to hang in."

Platt College is a two-year, proprietary (private) institution offering a diploma, certificate, and associate degree in graphic/computer design. Postassociate degree courses leading to a diploma in multimedia are also available.

"Most students go for the associate degree, which consists of four terms, 16 weeks each, for a total of 64 weeks," says Randy Mastronicola, Director of Admissions and Marketing. "With term one, it's the basics: design and pre-press. In term two, we move on to the computer with an introduction to computer drawing, painting, and page layout programs. Term three covers computer design and production: advanced skills in Illustrator, Photoshop, and QuarkXPress, as well as PageMaker and Freehand."

An additional term to complete general education requirements—the main factor distinguishing an associate degree from a certificate at any two-year school—is also necessary. Here students take courses such as English Composition, Art History, Psychology, and Interpersonal Communications.

Once you have the associate degree, you're eligible to take one or two terms in advanced multimedia. That's what Kim Brestow finds herself doing, as she sits before a Mac G3 with its two color monitors. "I use one monitor to display my toolbars," she says. "The other is for my viewing space."

Kim is learning ImageReady 2.0, a program that allows her to create simple flip-book animations. After drawing and coloring a cartoon figure, she animates it. "I duplicate the figure a half-dozen times, then click the mouse," she says. "Presto, the little character jumps around."

Kim, the mother of a nine-year-old, is hoping for a job in animation or special effects.

"I have done art all my life," she declares, "but after high school, it was party, party, party. I just wasn't ready to get serious. Now I am. With knowledge and skill in graphic design, I figure the doors should open up."

Where do those doors lead?

Here are a few entry-level job titles open to those with a certificate or degree from a postsecondary institution like Platt College:

- Advertising Designer

- Art Director's Assistant

- Print Production Assistant

- 2-D, 3-D Animator

- Web Designer

- Service Bureau Specialist

- Photograph Manipulation, Color Correction Specialist

- Studio Designer

- Production/Camera Ready Artist

- Commercial Artist

- Digital Graphic Designer

- Illustrator

- Multimedia Designer

- Digital Colorist

- Mac Artist

- Production Designer

- Electronic Artist

All require education and training, however, the kind you can get from a two-year college, public or private.

A GRAND ACADEMY

Santa Monica College is a two-year California community college, the main campus located less than a mile from the beach on which episodes of *Baywatch* are regularly filmed. Sun, sand, and surf, plus excellent academic programs, have attracted 30,000 students to this institution. That and an unbelievably low tuition—$11 dollars per unit.

A few blocks from the main campus, in the city's emerging West End post-production mecca, sits a two-story, 12,000-square-foot former office building now housing the college's Academy of Entertainment and Technology. Established in 1997 with the support of industry partners such as Warner Brothers Television, Sony Interactive, Lucas Digital, Ltd., Walt Disney Imagineering, DreamWorks SKG, Digital Domain, and Capital Records, the academy has little trouble attracting its own group of students.

"While most come from the local area, we get quite a few from all over the country—Colorado, Illinois, even back east," says Judith Penchansky, Assistant Dean of Student Affairs for External Programs. "Of course, out-of-state and foreign students pay considerably more to attend—$133 a unit."

Though getting into a community college in California is as easy as turning eighteen or having a high school diploma, being allowed to work toward a certificate or associate degree in Animation or Interactive Media at the academy demands more.

"We require an essay and a portfolio," says Judith. "Last semester 150 portfolios were submitted for review. Half the applicants were admitted into the program."

In writing the essay, students are asked to respond to the following:

- Briefly state what you expect to gain from attending the Academy of Entertainment and Technology.

- What can you offer the Santa Monica College Academy community?

- Describe any extracurricular activities or hobbies as they relate to your goals.

- Tell us about any specialized training, internship, or employment that has given you experience in art, design, animation, interactive media, business, or the entertainment industry.

- Where do you see yourself in five years?

What does the academy look for in a portfolio?

In general, applicants must submit their best, most recent work. The portfolio should represent their personal interests and abilities. Advisors look for a spark of drawing ability and creativity that can be demonstrated by including landscapes, still life, animals, design work, something in color, photos, or life drawings.

For an interactive media portfolio they like pieces that exhibit a grasp of complex issues or an individual point of view or a unique approach to a problem using typography and imagery. They are not looking for professionals. On the other hand, they don't want true beginners who might bring the rest of the students down.

To be sure, Antonella Pozzo-Ardizzi, a forty-four-year-old student from Italy whose background includes scenic painting for Disney in France, fashion design in Milan, and choreography for Club Med, isn't bringing any standards down at the Academy; she's raising them. "All that traditional background is helpful in my animation studies," she says. "Animators should know choreography, acting, voice, theater. After all, it's all about telling a story."

There you have it: two two-year institutions, Platt College and Santa Monica College. One is private, the other public. Being in Southern California, and less than 30 miles from Hollywood, no wonder they offer (in addition to regular programs in art and graphic design) specialties in animation and multimedia.

Yet the same can be said for many such schools all across the country. You don't have to live and study in the motion picture capital to pursue a career in these and other art-related fields. Let's get a sampling of what is happening around the country, on the East Coast and in the Midwest.

EXTREME SIGNAGE

The Butera School of Art in Boston, Massachusetts is one of the few art schools in the country offering an extensive program in sign painting. A two-year (1,800-hour) diploma course is available to those who are at least seventeen years old, hold a high school diploma or equivalent certificate (GED), and can afford the steep tuition, approximately $11,000 a year. Yet, accredited by the Accrediting Commission of Career Schools and Colleges of Technology (ACCSCT), Butera is an institution where you get what you pay for. It has been teaching sign painting since 1910.

"Our endeavor is to graduate students who can design and letter functional and aesthetically pleasing signs, trucks, vans, murals, and boats," says Joseph Butera, the school's president. "It is an art that requires talent and training, the latter in both tractional skills and computer know-how."

The market for such aptitude is varied and growing. Today you can see practical application of signs in television, movies, promotions, displays, billboards, office doors, windows, charts, posters, and, of course, vans and trucks. You have signage for boats, race cars, custom cars, and funny cars. And extreme sports enthusiasts as well as professional sports organizations are looking to sign painters to customize their equipment.

Since most applicants to the Butera School of Art have no prior instruction in sign lettering, a portfolio is not required. Furthermore, loans, scholarships, and grants are available.

Interested? Contact the school at (617) 536-4623; *www.buteraschool.com*.

READY TO JOIN THE CIA?

Everyone knows what the CIA is; it's the Central Intelligence Agency. But it is also the Connecticut Institute of Art, a two-year professional career school dedicated exclusively to commercial art, located in Greenwich, Connecticut. Advertising and graphic design, computer graphics, airbrush, illustration, and figure drawing are covered extensively.

"Our program involves what we call Pigments to Pixels," says Mike Propersi, the school's president. "While we recognize the importance of using the most modern of tools for design—the computer—it is no substitute for art and design knowledge. The computer does not do things well; it only does them fast. There's no design key on the keyboard."

Like most institutions of its kind, the CIA requires you to be a high school graduate or equivalent and present a portfolio to gain admission. Actually, the portfolio is something the CIA emphasizes not only for admission but also for graduation.

"From the very first day at the CIA, you will hear about your portfolio," says Mike. "And throughout your education here you will constantly be evaluating, redoing, building, and re-creating it over and over again. The portfolio is the single most important element in beginning and advancing your career as a commercial artist."

For more information on the CIA, call (800) 278-7246.

ADVERTISE IT LOUD AND CLEAR

The School of Advertising Art, located in Kettering, Ohio, is a two-year proprietary college/art school that, as its name indicates, prepares students for careers in advertising art. Offering both a diploma and an associate degree, the SAA covers all aspects of advertising art including graphic design, illustration, computer animation, marketing, English, art history, and creative writing.

What will you be prepared for once you graduate?

"Students, upon graduation, have the necessary skills for entry-level positions in advertising such as graphic designer, illustrator, and Mac production artist," says Tim Potter, founder and director of the SAA. "They go on to design and illustrate brochures, annual reports, logos, packages, newspaper and magazine ads, and other types of advertising including multimedia, TV commercials, and animation.

"It is important to remember what graphic designers are," adds Tim. "They are skilled observers who find solutions to communications challenges. Creatively assessing and establishing the best balance between diverse elements is what a graphic designer is trained to do."

The SAA can be reached at (937) 294-0592; *www.saacollege.com.*

CREATIVITY, THAT'S WHAT IT IS ALL ABOUT

Creativity! That term keeps coming up whenever careers in art and graphic design are mentioned. That's understandable; creativity is completely interwoven into the design process.

Can it be taught? Perhaps not. But it can be fostered—made to grow. Remember, more than just coming up with ideas, the creative process is fertilizing, pruning, ripening, and harvesting them.

Above all, when choosing an institution to pursue your studies in art and graphic design, you must select one where your creativity will be encouraged. Consider these thoughts and questions, developed by Roger Hubbard for a college recruiting brochure:

- *Creativity is seeing what everyone else has seen and thinking what no one else has thought.* Thus, will the education and training you seek refine your vision and teach you to be an independent thinker?

- *Creativity does not emerge from a state of relaxation but rather from a state of chaos.* Will you, at the institution you attend, be asked to work hard and juggle several projects at one time?

- *Studies show that creative people have an unusual capacity to record and report experiences.* Will the school you attend teach you the mechanics of picture making, improve your writing and speaking skills, and encourage you to keep a sketchbook to record your imagination?

- *Creative people do not readily accept rules and regulations.* Thus, will you be given rules so that you understand a structure for visual problem solving? Will you be held to such rules until you show that you can be creative within them? Will you then be asked to break the rules, as artists do?

Find a school that puts creativity and its encouragement above all else, and everything else will follow.

ASKING THE RIGHT QUESTIONS

In a recent web poll conducted by *How Magazine*, readers were asked: "Are design schools adequately preparing students for the professional world?" The results, published in the June 2000 issue of the magazine, were disquieting: 21 percent said yes; 79 percent, no. One reader responded, "Students are taught the glories of conceptual design, yet rarely are they adequately taught the tools with which to execute those concepts." Another declared, "Students seem surprised that the business isn't all black turtlenecks and redesigning IBM's identity, and that a one-color gig for Joe's House of Motor Oil pays the bills." Reality check time!

When attempting to select a postsecondary institution for art and graphic design studies, you must look around and ask the right questions. If you are visiting a campus:

- *Note the surrounding atmosphere.* Is the campus peaceful or overly rushed?

- *Visit the library.* Is it a quiet place with a wide variety of learning aids at the students' disposal?

- If possible, *sit in on one or more classes.* Observe both the instructor's approach and the students' responses.

- *Talk with students;* try to get a feel for what they think about the school. Look beyond what they say to their expressions of enthusiasm (or lack of it).

- *Pay attention to what's going on* and ask lots of questions. Be assertive.

- *Find out about extracurricular programs.* Are there any you may want to become involved in?

Of course, you will also want to know about internships, job placement, financial aid, and whether the institution is accredited and by whom. It's an exciting time—choosing a career and the best way to pursue it. Select wisely; your life's work depends on it.

SCHOOLS THAT ARE DOING IT

Here is a sampling of two-year, postsecondary schools offering programs in art and graphic design taken from the Siggraph (Special Interest Group on

Computer Graphics) web site:
http://www.siggraph.org/cgi-bin/education/search.pl
 For a complete listing, visit the web site.

Art Institutes
1900 Yorktown
Houston, TX 77056
(713) 623-2040
Web site: *http://www.aih.aii.edu*
The Art Institutes is a family of schools offering associate degrees in design, media arts and technology, fashion, and culinary arts. There are campuses in Atlanta, Dallas, Ft. Lauderdale, Houston, Los Angeles, Philadelphia, Phoenix, Pittsburgh, Seattle, Portland, and San Francisco, among other locations.

Cabrillo Community College Desktop Publishing and Multimedia Program
6500 Soquel Drive
Aptos, CA 95003
(831) 479-6400
Web site: *http://www.cabrillo.cc.ca.us/*
Desktop Publishing and Multimedia offers courses in the technology and skills needed for entry-level employment and preparation for advanced specialized courses in the fields of digital publishing for printed media, and for multimedia production.

Center for Digital Imaging and Sound
3264 Beta Avenue
Burnaby, Canada, V5G4K4
(800) 661-1885
Web site: *http://www.artschool.com*
The center offers one- and two-year programs in classical animation, 3-D animation, and visual effects animation. Students study both traditional and classical animation techniques.

Colorado Institute of Art

200 East Ninth Street
Denver, CO 80203
(303) 837-0825
Web site: *http://www.cia.aii.edu*
The Colorado Institute offers both a bachelor's degree and an associate degree, the latter in fashion design, graphic design, photography, multimedia and web design, and video production.

Miami-Dade Community College Film and Video

11380 NW 27th Avenve
Miami, FL 33167
(305) 237-1566
    This college offers a four-course sequence of computer graphics/animation for film and production and TV broadcast students. There are also courses in graphic arts computer graphics, architecture, and engineering computer-aided design (CAD).

Raritan Valley Community College Fine and Performing Arts

PO Box 3300
North Branch, NJ 08876
(908) 218-8876
Web site: *http://www.raritanval.edu*
    Raritan Valley Community College awards associate of arts degrees in liberal arts and fine arts preparing students to transfer into the junior year of study toward bachelor's degrees in a variety of art majors. The A.A. degrees are designed for transfer and include the visual arts options: graphic design and studio arts.

Springfield College Art Department

263 Alden Street
Springfield, MA 01109
(413) 748-3679
Web site: *http://www.spfdcol.edu/homepage.nsf*

Computer graphics is a new major at Springfield College. This hands-on program emphasizes three main areas of study: three-dimensional animation, multimedia/video, and graphic design.

Valencia Community College, Department of Graphics Technology
701 N. Econlockhatchee Trail
Orlando, FL 32825
(407) 299-5000
Web site: *http://www.gate.net/~valencia/*

The Graphic Design Technology program prepares students for employment as designers, commercial artists, and computer graphic designers. Digital Prepublishing Technology prepares students for employment in computerized layout, prepress production, and entry-level multimedia graphics.

A FEW KEY POINTS TO REMEMBER

- You don't need a bachelor's degree to enter the fields of art and graphic design.
- You must be both educated and trained in the arts.
- Portfolios rather than résumés are what the industry looks for when evaluating a potential employee.
- A portfolio should contain your best, most recent work.
- Proprietary schools are private and charge a relatively high tuition, though loans, scholarships, and grants are available.
- More than 1,300 postsecondary institutions offer certificates, diplomas, or associate degrees in art and art-related fields.
- You don't have to study in Hollywood to pursue a career in animation or multimedia.
- The computer does not have a design key on the keyboard.
- Every postsecondary art school should encourage creativity above all else.
- When visiting a prospective campus, pay attention to what is going on and ask lots of questions.

CHAPTER FOUR

Artists and Illustrators

F unction is out. Form is in. From radios to cars to toothbrushes, America is crazy about design, according to a *Time Magazine* article, "The Rebirth of Design," March 20, 2000. And, as Alan Swann, renowned designer and author of numerous books in the field, reminds us, "We should be aware of the increasing relevance of design as part of the artistic and cultural development of the society in which we live. Good design, communicating good services or products, is becoming the cornerstone of our society."

If design is in, then so is the designer. Indeed, according to the *Time Magazine* article, nimble, jack-of-all-trades designers are emerging, knocking down the walls between architecture, industrial products, and graphic design, turning out everything from cars to can openers. It's an exciting time to be in art and graphic design. It's not a Rodney Dangerfield field anymore— designers *do* get respect.

WHAT IS A GRAPHIC ARTIST/GRAPHIC DESIGNER?

As we have discovered, a graphic artist is an artist working in a commercial arena. A graphic designer is an artist who labors with the elements of typography, illustration, photography, and printing to create commercial communications tools such as advertisements, brochures, signage, posters, slide shows, book jackets, and other forms of printed or graphic communications. Designers are visual problem solvers.

One aspect of graphic design—one we identify most with the profession—is art and illustration. The illustrator is a professional graphic artist who communicates a pictorial idea by creating a visual image using paint, pen, pencil, collage, or any graphic technique except the photograph.

In this chapter we look closely at four fields in which artists and illustrators work.

1. We examine, first, the careers of animator and game designer, discovering how exciting yet challenging both these related endeavors can be.

2. Next, we see where the specialized and celebrated field of fashion illustration is going. While the profession's glory days are over, those who illustrate the draped body still find work, often in surprising places.

3. Sign graphic artists, using computer-generated vinyl, are literally painting the town, throwing their work up on windows, trucks, billboards, anywhere that art-by-the-yard is needed. We'll check them out.

4. Book illustration has matured in recent years; no longer is it just jacket covers and baby board books. From illustrated handouts for kindergartners to enhancing the most recent young adult thriller, illustrators of books and educational materials are busy, indeed.

So, let's get started. It's time to examine careers in which drawing it up is what it's all about.

ANIMATION AND GAME DESIGN: NOT ALL PLAYTIME

By contorting his mouth, squinting his eyes, thrusting his tongue out, and gritting his teeth, Colm Duggan of Rich Animation Studios sees in the mirror above his desk what he needs to draw on his light table.

"You make a face, then caricature that shape," says Colm, whom we met briefly in Chapter One. "Everything in animation is exaggerated to get the right effect. This is particularly true with facial expressions. I can't help but look at myself."

AN EXPLODING FIELD

An animator (one who draws animated cartoons, whether with traditional pencil and paper or, increasingly, by computer) works in a collaborative industry with a diverse team.

- First, there are *script writers* who create the story line.

- Next, *art directors* design the characters, setting the look and style.

- *Storyboard artists* then lay out animation cels, "frozen" images of selected scenes.

- Finally, *animators* draw each frame.

Animation itself has many parts.

When done using traditional methods, there are *pencilers* who draw each character for each frame, *inkers* who ink over the pencil drawings, *colorers* who fill in the inked drawings, and *cleanup artists* who make sure items like the fairy princess's hair are consistent throughout in style, shape, and color.

"In many studios," says Steve Fossati of Chuck Jones Productions, "animators do only certain kinds of scenes. For example, there are those who can draw only backgrounds, scenes with little animation. Or, we have animators who just want to do action scenes: soaring flights, swinging off ropes, and such. Finally, effects animators draw splashes, smoke, mud flying, and objects exploding. It all depends on your expertise and interest."

Animation is an exploding field for artists, male and female, because there is a commitment to animation across the board, from standard feature films to CD-ROMs, from multimedia to the Internet. And remember, with the downturn in the aerospace industry a few years ago, all those CAD operators were out looking for work. They found it in the world of computer animation.

A FIELD IN MOTION

Despite the natural shakeout occurring in the industry, animators (especially those comfortable with the computer, running SoftimagToonz, U.S. Animation, Flash, Shockwave, and practically anything produced by Avid) are finding plenty to do. To illustrate, here are two job ads from the Animation World Network's Career Connection's hotline:

- New York City-based Nickelodeon Animation Studio is seeking talented professionals for their TV series "Little Bill," a breakthrough 26-part TV animation series based on the books written by Bill Cosby for preschool children. Nickelodeon is seeking talented After Effects Character Animators, Storyboard Artists, Traditional Animators, and Digital Design/Ink and Paint.

- Chicago-suburbs-based Terraglyph Interactive Studios is looking for talented and creative people to join the 50-strong staff currently producing high-quality, original, and licensed game titles for PC, Sony PlayStation and PlayStation 2, Sega Dreamcast, and Nintendo Dolphin. Experienced Animators, In-Between, and Clean Up Artists wanted. Also experienced Illustrators wanted.

From traditional artists to special effects modelers and game designers, animation is a field in motion.

CHICK GAME CHAMP

Speaking of game design, playing Donkey Kong on Nintendo 64 may become homework if you're a student in the University of California at Irvine's newest concentration: the Interdisciplinary Gaming Studies Program, according to the *Wall Street Journal*. The program will explore the growing role of video games as well as teach students the technical skills to program and design the computer pastimes.

Stevie Case, who we introduced in Chapter One, didn't major in game studies in college, yet the exuberant twenty-two-year-old female game designer, also known as the Cyber world's First Chick Game Champ for having beaten her boss, John Romero, at his own game of Quake, is making her mark in this art-based genre that has now outstripped theater attendance in revenue, reaching $7.45 billion in 1999.

"After college, I spent two years freelancing from my home in Dallas," Stevie says. "I did level design using tools I found on the Net for free. Then I saw an ad for a play tester at Ion Storm. Sure, it was an entry-level job, but it got me in the door where I could play with their Level editor."

Though there are talented artists and game designers earning six-figure incomes and putting in 70 to 80 hours a week to do so, most in the field aren't getting rich.

"You don't want to do this if your ultimate focus is to make money," says Stevie. "Instead, zero in on creating a fun game. Build your portfolio. Sacrificing the financial side first will pay off in the end."

Good advice when pursuing any career in art and graphic design.

FASHION ILLUSTRATION: DRAWING THE DRAPED BODY

Fashion illustrators are artists who love fashion. No question, their profession is in trouble. Some say it is dying; others claim it is already dead. For sure, the glory days of fashion illustration, where newspapers and magazines filled their ad pages with fabulously clad women to lure customers into Bullocks-Wilshire, Bloomingdale's, and Saks Fifth Avenue, are gone. It seems commissions are fewer, deadlines are shorter, and fees are lower. But work is still being done and, according to those who should know, an upswing is occurring.

LOOKING GOOD

"It's coming back," says Sharon Tate, former associate dean of the acclaimed fashion program at Los Angeles Trade Technical College and coauthor of *The Complete Book of Fashion Illustration*. "People are getting tired of photography. Besides, no matter how accurate a picture is, accuracy is not always what it's about. Making people look better than they really are is the illustrator's forte. That will always have appeal."

Unlike regular descriptive drawing, fashion drawing does not aim for realism. Rather, current ideals of beauty are emphasized to create a stylized, exaggerated version of reality. To create good fashion drawings, the illustrator must understand the current ideal of beauty and how clothing is used to enhance the human body.

Mona Shafer Edwards, Sharon's coauthor on a half-dozen books including *The Complete Book of Fashion Illustration*, warns: "It's tough out there. If students think they're going to graduate from a two-year school, or any school for that matter, and begin drawing costumes for Diana Ross—forget it. This is a tough, competitive field where only the best can earn a living."

BEYOND FASHION

Mona, like many in the business—and it *is* a business—finds additional ways to use her fashion illustration talent.

"I do courtroom drawings for ABC," she says. "Most of the illustrations done for the O.J. Simpson trial were my work."

Fashion illustration taught Mona how to draw the draped body and to do it fast. She doesn't pigeonhole herself; nor must you. If you want to do fashion illustration, look around for related work.

Gregory Werquiton, a freelancer, did just that. After more than 35 years in the profession, he now spends considerable time doing comp art (comprehensive art that is usually created for the client and artist to use as a guide for the finished art).

"I've never made so much money," he says. "Comp art isn't published, but it's great work."

Indeed! Studio executives want a concept drawing for a new movie, for example. The director tells you what he has in mind and you draw a picture of a head from the nose down, mouth open, tongue licking a fork. The only way to present that kind of concept is to have someone sketch it.

If you choose to do fashion illustration, expect rough going, but if you keep attuned to related opportunities, any that involve drawing the dressed body, you can find opportunities in fashion illustration.

SIGNAGE EVERYWHERE: ART BY THE YARD

As we saw in Chapter Three, sign graphics, art-by-the-yard, is everywhere: windows, office doors, billboards, posters, movies, television, in-store displays, extreme sports equipment, boats, and, of course, vehicles. Coming up with the right sign design, then executing it in an attractive and professional manner, requires creativity and skill. Anatole Paquette of Paquette Signs in Meredith, New Hampshire has been doing so for 25 years.

"It is a creative process," he says. "The customer starts out wanting a sign, but hasn't a clue as to what he's looking for. You visit his site, whether it is a motel, an office, or a restaurant, and you create a logo for starters. Soon it is on to business cards, stationery, checks, a Yellow Page ad—the works. You are building an identity for him. Before you know it, he needs job signs, office signs, vehicle signs, silk-screened jackets, and embroidered caps. You keep growing with his business."

COMPUTER-GENERATED SIGNS

As in all areas of art and graphic design, the computer has impacted sign graphics, in this case in the form of CGS—computer-generated signs.

"Our traditional hand skills are going by the board," says Ralph (Doc) Guthrie, a professor of sign graphics. "When I came to my college ten years ago, it was 90 percent handwork. Now it is the other way around, 90 percent computers. We use Gerber Graphixs Advantage and SignLab to design and print out vinyl letters from one-tenth of an inch to ten inches."

However, traditional skills are still in demand.

"Sign graphic artists need design skills," adds Doc. "They must know letter construction, spacing, color, and pattern. We're like all commercial artists; we just do large format design.

"I find people designing signs who can't name the font they're using," bemoans Doc. "They scroll through a menu on the computer screen, see something they like, and hit the print key. It's so cookie-cutter."

Edwin Saravia is a twenty-four-year-old full-time sign graphics designer at his local Home Depot store.

"They don't want me designing on a computer," he says. "I can do both, freehand and on the computer, but they like the hand-lettered look. Believe me, the freehand approach is not dead."

Demand for sign graphic artists is so high that many students aren't finishing their training program.

"With all the price changes, merchandise sales, banners, and educational material required on a daily basis, most Home Depot stores have a full-time sign painter," says Doc. "Their managers come around recruiting students right out of my program—in the second semester, no less."

That's unfortunate. Students who leave Doc's program early miss out on his important fourth semester's business module.

AVENUE FOR THE SELF-EMPLOYED

The real money in this field is in self-employment. Opening your own shop is the key. You can begin working out of your room, garage, basement—whatever. Pretty soon you're in business for yourself, full time.

"Many of our graduates work for someone else for awhile, then start their own business," says Joseph Butera, of the Butera School of Art. "It's terrific. It offers kids independence."

And the need for sign graphics is always there, in the good times as well as the bad.

After all, even Going Out of Business signs are necessary. When Braniff Airlines was grounded a few years back, the company didn't take those planes to the dump. The new owners repainted them.

BOOK ILLUSTRATION: BEYOND THE WRITTEN WORD

Book illustrators work inside and out to tell a story visually.

Such illustrators have long been recognized as an important ingredient in the editorial and marketing value of a book. They work with editors, art directors, book designers, or book packagers to create anything from simple instructional line drawings to full-color-spread illustrations for textbooks, young adult books, picture books, and special reprints of classics, among other categories.

Book jacket illustration or design, according to many, is the second most important ingredient in the promotion and sale of a book, superseded only by the fame and success of the author.

SHE'S GOT A STYLE

Even with the monumental changes taking place within the publishing industry, consolidation and electronic publishing being only two, illustrators are still needed to do what words cannot—illustrate the message.

"What I do is quite simple," says Deborah Zemke of Columbia, Missouri. "I draw."

A freelance book illustrator for 15 years, Deborah spends about half her time illustrating for children: books, magazines, and educational materials. She has also illustrated, mostly in line drawing, Barron's *Business Success* series.

"For the most part, I work in a humorous style," she says. "In the *Business Success* series, there were 20 books with 30 illustrations each. That's 600 illustrations to help enliven the reading experience, add a little warmth."

Bob Staake, of St. Louis, Missouri, also a freelance illustrator, does lots of illustrating for the children's market. He has illustrated more than 25 books, including the popular Simon & Schuster *My Little . . .* book series. Yet, Bob is a generalist first, willing to do illustrations for magazines, greeting cards, advertising brochures, plus animation stills and the usual corporate stuff.

"I believe the key to my success is diversity," he explains. "Fortunately, I'm an illustrator with a style applicable in many areas."

GO HAVE FUN WITH IT

Priscilla Burris, a self-taught freelance illustrator, specializes almost exclusively in children's works.

"Mainly it's educational material, from sheets handed out to children in kindergarten to help them with their numbers, to beautifully illustrated literature books," she says. "With the former, the publisher tells me specifically what he wants: an Asian girl, seven years old, wearing glasses, walking down the street with her grandmother. With the books, I have more freedom. I'm there to help tell the story at critical moments."

You'd think that children's book illustrators would work closely with the author, the better to get a shared vision across. Not so!

"I talk only to art directors and editors, never the author," says Priscilla. "Sometimes I don't even know who the author is until the book is published. The writer has his or her own vision, and so does the illustrator. Editors keep us apart."

"I tend to be given a manuscript and told to 'Go have fun with it'," adds Bob. "In most cases I never deal with the author. In fact, I do not recall an author ever thanking me for my contribution, even after the book is published."

Like most illustrators, those doing books are finding the computer a necessary tool.

"Since 1995 I have been entirely on the computer," says Bob. "I use Photoshop on a Mac for all my illustrations. I upload illustrations to my server and the art director downloads them to his. No FedEx or U.S.P.S. mail to worry about."

IT'S A BUSINESS

Because most illustrators work freelance, being a good businessperson is as important as knowing their art, maybe more so.

"In this business, and it *is* a business," says Bob, "the business end is even more important than the art. Artists will always find a way to make the art work, assuming they have the talent and skill. But though many artists will bristle at my comments, to succeed you must know how to negotiate, get what you deserve. Editors and art directors will respect you for it."

Respect is something all book illustrators want. Unfortunately, not all approach their work in a manner that assures they'll get it.

"Professionalism is crucial," says Bob. "I do not do this to get my name on a book cover. I do not illustrate children's books so I can visit the grade school down the street and say, 'Here's my book.' While I love my work, it is work. It is my livelihood. I have to support a family. I need the income. I do it for the money."

ILLUSTRATION: A DIVERSE FIELD

We have seen artists and illustrators at work in four fields: animation and game design, fashion illustration, sign graphics, and book illustration. Related fields abound: architectural illustrator, background artist, billboard designer, calligrapher, cartoonist, comic book creator, comic strip artist, greeting card designer, marine illustrator, medical illustrator, renderer, tattoo artist, technical illustrator, type designer, visual aids artist, and police artist.

By way of illustration—no pun intended—consider that New York City now has 3,000-plus bus shelters, each sporting two 46- by 47-inch glass-enclosed posters that are rotated, more or less, on a monthly basis. As famed graphic designer Steve Heller has noted, "Six thousand illuminated posters have had a decisive impact not only on the public's consciousness but on designers, too." The added employment opportunities are, indeed, encouraging.

In examining careers in art and illustration, three themes emerge.

1. Some artists and illustrators are barely into the computer, if at all. Others can't imagine doing their art without it. Most are in between, but clearly looking for ways to enhance what they do with this digital tool.

2. Most illustrators, by choice or because there is no other choice, work for themselves as freelancers. For them, the business end of

their day is as important as the art they do. We will examine the freelancing world in depth in Chapter Nine.

3. While specialization has its advantages, few artists and illustrators can make a living in a specific field. Diversity is the key to survival in these rewarding, but competitive, careers.

COMPANIES THAT ARE DOING IT

Here are a few companies specializing in the work artists and illustrators do:

Cheryl Mendenhall
http://www.nashville.net/~mendenmh/portfolio.html
Nashville-based artist who specializes in computer-assisted illustration with children's themes.

Chester Lake Creations
http://www.chesterlake.com/
Design firm that specializes in designing web pages and creating banners and logos.

Alien Grafix
http://www.se.mediaone.net/~grafix/
Produces designs for web sites, comic books, illustrations, tattoos, and photography.

Always Open
http://207.94.34.33/Graphics/
San Ramon, California company that offers web site graphics, logos, corporate images, business cards, and ads.

People
Who Are Doing It

MEET JIM KESSHEM

VITAL STATISTICS

Jim Kesshem, a forty-five-year-old storyteller, is head of Jim Kesshem Productions. He is working on a variety of commercial animation projects.

❏ PRESENT JOB

Full-time teaching and since 1976 president of Jim Kesshem Productions. His responsibility is to create characters, personalities, and stories to be pitched to such entities as Nickelodeon and the Cartoon Network.

❏ TRADITION

"I am more of a traditional animator," says Jim. "I have not gotten heavy into the computer like everyone else. As a result, I'm sort of passé. But since I know people in the business—principals, chief animators, storyboarders, in-betweeners, and plenty who can flash their way around Flash—I am in demand. I know how the business works. Besides, just because you are fancy with the computer doesn't make you a fabulous animator. Nonetheless, anyone getting into the field now must know how to move a mouse as well as a pen."

❏ **TELLING A STORY**

Jim teaches a course on storytelling. It is a subject at the core of what animation is about and needs to be. Here's an abbreviated description:

This introductory course covers storytelling fundamentals. The course follows the path of storytelling through the ages, beginning with an overview of the history of story from its roots of pictorial and oral tradition, to its modern form of entertainment, the movies, the Internet, and computer games.

"Everyone tells a story," says Jim. "Doctors, lawyers, architects. It is central to everything we do in animation."

MEET ROBERT PASSANTINO

VITAL STATISTICS

Robert Passantino, fifty-two, is a freelance fashion illustrator based in New York City. In his 34 years in the field, he has created fashion illustrations for Bloomingdale's, Playboy Magazine, *countless newspapers, the weekly* Tobbe Report, *and web sites such as* Alight.com. *It has always been his dream to work in this profession.*

❏ **PRESENT JOB**

Freelance fashion illustrator working in New York.

❏ PRESENTING A CONCEPT

"It's not all photographs," Robert says. "Believe me, we are seeing illustrations being used again. Remember, a key purpose of an illustration is to sell a concept. Furthermore, often a designer doesn't have merchandise ready. I have to illustrate the concept. I've done that sort of thing, working just from a phone description. There's no other way to do it but through illustration."

In the end, it's knowing how clothes fall on the body. Can you draw a *croquis* (pronounced cro-key), a rough sketch for fashion illustration? It must accurately show the silhouette and style details. The collar, cuffs, and trims must be drawn to scale so the actual garment can be constructed in fabric.

"While photographs can do a job," Robert says, "advertisers have always known that buyers project themselves better into an illustration than a photograph. True, photographs are cheaper and faster, but when the whole point is to get you into the store, what does it matter?"

❏ COMPUTER MODIFICATION

"I like the computer," Robert says, "but I'm not overly fascinated by it. I scan an illustration and then work in Photoshop to enhance its color, shade, line emphasis, etc. I have tried doing the basic illustration on the computer but it feels stiff. Fluidity—flow—is a problem. Besides, many art directors don't want work solely done on a computer. Artists who do so take a very different approach with different results. It needs to look hand drawn."

❏ GLAMOROUS IT AIN'T

"I have worked for Calvin Klein, Versace, you name them," Robert volunteers. "There is nothing glamorous about it. If you think, 'Wow, I'm going to be involved in all these shows, go to all these fabulous functions,' forget it. This is work, not play. Fashion illustration is a serious business."

MEET JANE LANDWARE

VITAL STATISTICS

Jane Landware, thirty-eight, spent ten years in the restaurant business before the long hours got to her. Then a friend who owned an event production company asked Jane to make some signs for her. In exchange, the friend gave Jane space at her company to pursue the sign business. Today, Jane has a small, 550-square-foot shop, Sign Solutions, and is her own boss. Working fewer hours and enjoying it more, Jane will make more money this year than she ever did as a restaurateur.

❏ PRESENT JOB

Owner of Sign Solutions.

❏ MY SIGNS WERE AWFUL

"Starting your own sign business is easy; it takes only a minimum investment," says Jane. "But succeeding, primarily by designing and making great signs, is another matter."

As Jane got started, doing signs for her friend, she soon realized how little she knew. "I said, 'Gosh, my signs don't look very good. I don't know what I'm doing.'"

That's when she found a program at her local community college. "I went full time for two years, 7:00 A.M. to 12:00 noon, while working at the event production company in the afternoon," Jane says.

At her college she was both inspired and intimidated.

"I looked around and saw all these students doing beautiful hand lettering. 'They're artists,' I thought. 'How can I ever compete with them?'"

But Jane had the desire to improve—to create a better-looking sign. "It doesn't matter how talented you are if you aren't doing anything with it," she says. "I was out to succeed."

❏ IT'S A BUSINESS, TOO

With a two-year certificate in hand, Jane had the confidence to leave her corner at the event production company and open her own shop.

"I now felt I could sell my stuff," she says. "The first year was slow, but then the business kicked into gear. I soon realized that I can make a living at this without working 12-hour days—for someone else."

Today, Jane has taken on a partner with a background in imaging and color correcting on the computer. "She spent years in the printing industry," says Jane. "It's a great fit. I put her in charge of our digital art department."

Jane has advice for high school seniors contemplating a career in sign graphics: "It gives you an opportunity to make a great living where you don't have to worry about job security. Signs are something people will always need. They always want new information—new hours, promotional material, a different logo color. Change is great for my business."

MEET PHYLLIS POLLEMA-CAHILL

VITAL STATISTICS

Phyllis Pollema-Cahill, thirty-six, is a full-time illustrator working out of her home in Colorado Springs, Colorado. She specializes in the children's market, having illustrated for book publishers such as Shortland Publications, Star Bright Books, and the International Bible Society, as well as magazines such as Highlights for Children, Guideposts for Kids, The Friend, *and* Junior Trails/Discovery Trails. *Phyllis holds an associate degree in illustration from the Rocky Mountain College of Art and Design and is a member of the Society of Children's Book Writers and Illustrators. She is married to Jeff, a sign graphic artist.*

❏ NO ADULTS ALLOWED

Children's illustrators need special skills; it's not just enough to be able to draw people.

"First, you have to know how to draw kids of different age groups, different ethnicities," says Phyllis. "Knowing how to draw animals doesn't hurt either. But the main thing is to be sure your children don't look like little adults. When they do, it's scary."

❏ UP CLOSE AND PERSONAL

While Phyllis has all the software she needs to move from pen to mouse, she hasn't made the leap—yet. Her line drawings and colored art are done strictly the old fashioned way, by hand.

"I like the direct contact I get when putting pen to paper," she says. "The computer seems to set up a barrier for me. It doesn't totally emulate what I can do by hand. I like my art to be up close and personal."

❏ TURNING IT AWAY

Phyllis is in the enviable position where she is now earning a comfortable living as a freelance illustrator, though she is putting in 12-hour days, every day, to make it happen.

"To get freelancing to work, you have to know the business end," she declares. "You must be able to negotiate a decent price for your work and a contract on your terms. But right now my biggest challenge is managing my work load. My schedule is full enough; I have to learn to say No, I can't take that assignment."

As good as things are going for Phyllis, she insists she's not in the big leagues—not a superstar in the field.

"Those folks have a different day than I do," she points out. "They are the ones visiting schools, going on speaking engagements, and working strictly for royalties (a percentage of each book sold). And they're much more picky about the work they take on. I'm definitely not there yet."

Nonetheless, it is hard to call anyone a failure who is doing children's illustration exclusively, turning away business, and loving what she does. In any book, that is a success.

A FEW KEY POINTS TO REMEMBER

- Animation is exploding because there is commitment to the art form in many fields.
- There are talented artists and game designers earning six-figure incomes and putting in 70 to 80 hours a week to do so.
- If you choose fashion illustration, keep attuned to related opportunities.
- Sign artists need basic design skills to succeed; they must know letter construction, spacing, color, and pattern.
- As a sign graphic artist, think in entrepreneurial terms.
- Most illustrators work freelance. You must be a businessperson as well as an artist.

CHAPTER FIVE

Graphic Designers

"I realized that the only way to break out of price competition with premium waters was to design a striking new bottle," Robin Prever, CEO of the Saratoga Beverage Group, told a reporter in 1998. She then commissioned a sleek, flacon-shaped cobalt-blue glass bottle container. The design won the Glass Packaging Institute award and soon become a standard at upscale retailers and restaurants. Result: Company revenues increased more than 50 percent.

Graphic designers are practical artists whose creations are intended to be functional as well as attractive. They work with images (pictures) and letter forms to communicate a message. From gum wrappers to billboards and from bottles to the Web, in the design of books, brochures, packages, and business publications, their presence is everywhere. In computer graphics and multimedia, graphic designers with the right skills are in high demand. But once again, the basics are crucial. Familiarity with type, color, layout, and reproduction methods, whether they are print or electronic, are a must.

In this chapter we look at four careers requiring a graphic designer's sensibilities.

- Soon all businesses will have a web site. Designing attractive web pages that download quickly and that visitors return to again and again requires more than programming knowledge; it demands the services of a graphic designer.

- Commercial photographers make a living gathering images of everything from flowers to hubcaps, food to portraits. And with it all being reduced to 1's and 0's, with the resulting ease in image manipulation, photography and graphic design are converging. Enter the digital photographer as graphic designer.

- Package designers design primary and secondary packaging for all types of consumer products. Multidimensional and three-dimensional, such packaging must work at many levels. The way a customer interacts with the package is key. In the end, it is all about selling the product.

- Multimedia, or new media, interactive media, digital media—whatever it's called—is hot. Graphic designers in this field incorporate computer graphics, film, sound, and text to create everything from pure entertainment to products allowing users to navigate and manipulate information in an easily accessible manner.

WEB MANIA

If you can click a mouse you can design a web page—or so it would seem after perusing the many inexpensive web design software packages at your local office supplies retailer. Here are a few examples that promise you a web site in less than an hour, perhaps on your lunch break:

- *IXLA Webeasy: Complete Web Page Studio.* "A complete novice can create and publish a web page in less than an hour." Price: $62.97.

- *Web Studio 2.0.* "Easily create your own web site in minutes." Price: $35.97.

- *WebPage Construction Kit 5.0.* "Everything you need to easily create your own web pages." Price $22.48.

- *All-in-one Web Graphics.* "The software buy of the year." Price $49.97.

SO MUCH CLUTTER

None of this should be surprising; there's no doubting the need to design such pages. In the first 100 days of 1999, Internet usage doubled. And the World Wide Web (WWW), an organizing system within the Internet that makes it easy to establish links between computers, is the fastest-growing part of the Internet.

"As the millennium dawned, there were more than 5 million web sites in the world," says Brian Benson, president of Stellar City, a design and web posting company. "Total number of pages? One billion and climbing. There's plenty of work out there for those who can design and create these pages."

Yes, there is, for those who can do it well. The need for good design in a given medium has never been greater. "So much clutter exists out there, flashy this and that," says Mike Lejeune, a web site designer at KBDA, a 12-person design firm. "What's missing is web design based on good, solid principles: information organization, color theory, imagery, how to take someone visually through the message you are trying to get across."

Brent McMahan, of Sibley Peteet Design in Dallas, Texas, agrees: "Even on the Web, it's still about a story. If it is interactive, you are telling a story and someone is finishing it. Even though it is nonlinear, you must establish a rhythm—a sequence. Otherwise, it's like junk mail."

And it depends on the category of your web site, what type it is. Factors such as navigation, aesthetics, search, cutting-edge potential, and copy style will vary in emphasis with e-commerce, content, promotional, and portal sites. A good web page designer never forgets what it's all about, and why the site exists in the first place.

DODGER NEWS

Want to visit a terrific web site? Go to *www.dodgers.com*. Though you may not be a baseball fan, you'll immediately appreciate what great web site design is all about.

On a typical day, from the home page under Dodge News, you discover plans for stadium renovation. In the Press Box, you scroll through colorful logos that invite you to click on ticket information, Dodger merchandise, player information, and the season schedule. There are audio tips from coaches, games galore, contests to enter, and fan forums. Even text-based game updates—live—are available.

It's easy to see why, from its debut on April 24, 1996, this L.A. Dodger web site has conquered the charts, catching 41,000 to 50,000 discrete user sessions per day. *USA Today Baseball Weekly* gives the site a 9 for content, 9 for presentation, and 9.5 for bells and whistles—27.5 out of 30, way ahead of 29 other Major League sites scored.

For Steve Buchsbaum, president and CEO of Creative Edge Enterprises, Inc., a stat like that qualifies as a grand slam. "We began our fourth season with the Dodgers, designing, updating, and maintaining their web site," he says. "It's been a great growing experience."

THE WAY OF THE WORLD

What do you need to know, what design skills must you possess, to eventually do work of the type you've seen at the Dodger web site? To find out, one need only look at the seminar and workshop offerings at a typical web design conference, of which there are dozens around the country each year. Here are a few sample topics from the WEBLA Conference, held in Pasadena, California in May 2000:

- Evolution, not Revolution: The Past, Present, and Future of Web Design

- HTML Artistry: More than Code

- Introduction to Scalable Vector Graphics

- The Fine Art of Visual Design

- Seducing Your Audience with Shape and Color

- Writing for the Web

- Interactive On-line Training Design

- Cool CGI Tricks and Traps

- Java Enterprise Frameworks

- Introduction to Client-Side JavaScript

- Digital Storytelling

- Interactive Web 3-D Media

Even if you don't wish to specialize in web site design, as a graphic designer in the new millennium you will almost surely be a part of such design at some level. "It is the way of the world," says Mike. "Our firm is now doing 30 to 40 percent of its business in web design. Our clients—whether they are in packaging, corporate identity, advertising, or annual reports— expect us to include web site design as part of what we do, another service we offer. It is something all graphic designers need to get up to speed on."

A PHOTO OPPORTUNITY

The digital camera, which results in the ability to store and manipulate a filmless image, is revolutionizing the photography profession. Though the capital investment is still high, soon all professional photographers will go digital for at least some of their work.

Such photographers (using cameras to capture the mood that sells products, provides entertainment, highlights news stories, or brings back memories) are seeing a change in how they perform. Specializing in product, portrait, or media photography, digital photography, with its 1's and 0's, is changing everything. "Digital extends the opportunity for photographers," comments Dorie Ford, national executive director for the Advertising Photographers of America (APA). "It should be seen as another tool to both deliver and manipulate photographic images. All photography schools now teach the new technology."

GOING DIGITAL

And well they should. Photography's future, fine or commercial, may depend on it. It is predicted there will be 35 percent fewer freelance photographers in the next two to five years due to digital technology. But that doesn't necessarily mean there will be fewer photographs.

Nevertheless, the freelance photographic business is sure to diminish unless photographers are prepared to adjust to the future trends in the commissioning and purchasing of images. The industry is facing a major shake-up as a consequence of digital technology, but one can foresee this creating new opportunities that will enable photographers to diversify and carve out new careers for themselves rather than become redundant.

That's certainly what longtime photographer Ron Murry, at ImageActive, has done. Rather than see digital as a threat, his company has totally embraced the new medium. "It has transformed what we do, and not just because we have erased the cost of film," he says. "With digital, I can see immediately the results of my work. I know I have the shot. If not, I take it again until I get it."

MERGING OF ROLES

Digital photography has also resulted in the merging of traditional roles, particularly with regard to the photographer compared with the graphic designer. Everyone is now capable of using digital technology and is eager to defend their share of the market. Thus, no business is able to maintain a monopoly on the type of service it provides, because now, as a result of technology, they all have the means to do someone's else's job.

This convergence has long-term implications for photographers and their relationship with graphic designers. Whether working for an independent design firm, an in-house design department, an ad agency, or the client directly, photographers are being called upon to do work traditionally undertaken by their design colleagues—but it works both ways, as Ron found out. "My graphic designer friends are taking more photos, using the new technology," he says. "They don't need me as much. Yet, I can now do more of what they do. With photo manipulation software such as Photoshop, the careers of illustrator and photographer are merging. I'm becoming a graphic designer."

Still, most photographers want to be photographers first. They are, according to Jim Hagopian, president of APA Los Angeles, sticking to the tools that help them do just that: execute their photography. For sure, there is a cross section that is enthusiastic about digital, becoming more digitally oriented than others. For young people this can be particularly confusing. A whole different mind-set exists for shooting on film with its lighting and shadows, than for digital, which involves putting it into the computer and manipulating it, Jim maintains.

BRIGHT SHINY METAL

Jean Hill, whom we met earlier, in Chapter One, understands this all too well. Her bread-and-butter work involves bright, shiny metal. Known as a heavy-metal photographer by her friends, she has built a reputation photographing metal racing rims, all the time using film—for now anyway. "I have five clients," she says. "American Racing, TSW, Epic, GNC, and Beckman. No doubt soon they will be wanting everything in digital format."

Photographers are clearly an integral part of the graphic design team. Even if everyone can't do everyone else's job, everyone needs to know about what the other person does. It is an exciting time to be a photographer in the graphic design field. Great photo opportunities are everywhere—you just have to spot them.

A PACKAGE DEAL

Though often slaves to convention, package designers and food packagers in particular are, according to Steven Heller, challenging the commonplace. "'Eat me!' has in many cases been supplanted by 'Savor me!'" he says. "A relatively new breed of upscale food packaging is designed to be savored as much for the outside—artful appearance—as the inside." Thus, food is not only to be consumed, it is to be displayed, thanks to the work of graphic designers in general and package designers in particular.

Such packagers, whether in food, cosmetics, toys, or tools—you name it—work to protect, store, display, and promote a product's identity. There is both primary and secondary packaging, although what constitutes both varies within an industry. For example, in the beauty and fragrance field, primary means the bottle, jar, or container the product comes in. The secondary package is what the bottle or container goes into—a carton or box of some sort.

The only thing more important than the package is the product itself, one could argue. The package is its skin, its exterior facing. With some commodity-type products—soap flakes come quickly to mind—the package is the most important element.

CAPTIVATING AT A DISTANCE

What makes packaging design different from other forms of graphic design? Well, it's 3-D, of course, and that, naturally, introduces additional problems. Furthermore, a single package is one element out of many. Packaging design is multidimensional, interactive.

Keep in mind that a good package has to be captivating from a distance. It has to draw you in, work on many different levels. While it must have visual diversity, at the same time it needs to make sense. A lot of communication is involved. However, it is not all about being beautiful. Ultimately, a successful package is going to help sell the product.

To get there, many product-related factors need to be considered. It is important to bear in mind the kind of business involved and its distribution aspects. For example, how will the product fit on the shipping pallet? How is it to be handled, displayed on the shelf, and stacked? All these variables must be taken into account.

Then there's the all-important connection with the customer. Good package design must engage us on many levels, not the least of which is emotional. "Our focus is creating emotional connections among people, products, and brands," comments Phyllis Aragaki, of D/G New York. "So when it comes to packaging, we try to maximize the way we use materials—formal design elements, form, texture, color, typography—to give the package as much emotion as possible."

THINKING IN 3-D

Given these design factors, one would expect package designers to display characteristics necessary to produce such design. "What we look for is an understanding of three-dimensional work," says William Howard, of WL2 Design. "It comes down to basic design skills: great typography and a strong color sense. I don't think you have to specialize in packaging to do it. You just need to be a good designer—an intelligent and creative person."

In other words, a good package designer has the same skills as any designer: great sense of typography, color, form, line, and composition—things that are being skimmed over today in some cases because technology is so prevalent.

Tom Hough of Sibley Peteet Design got into packaging design for many reasons. While he admits there isn't much difference between doing brochures or boxes—"One is first cousin to the other," he says—he likes packaging design for its relatively long shelf life. "Let's face it, more people are going to see our beer bottle labels than a brochure for Northern Telecom. When I go into a restaurant and see everyone drinking beer with my label— well, that's pretty cool."

In the end, though, package designers are like all graphic designers; they must be educated in the basics and trained in the new tools, and they must be willing to do their apprenticeship—put in their time learning by doing. "As in any creative career," says Patrick Hunt of Hunt Adkins Studios, "you need to have the humility early on to get people's opinions and listen to those opinions and criticisms. It's hard to come out of school and just do it. Experience makes a huge difference. If you borrow from people's experiences, make adjustments in your work, you will accelerate a lot faster—in packaging design or any other creative endeavor."

MULTIMEDIA, MULTIPLE SKILLS

To many who have stood before it, neck strained at a 45-degree angle, the colossus of streaming technology is simply multimedia gone mad. The edifice, in New York's already visual-noise-saturated Times Square, is known as the NASDAQ Tower, officially the biggest monitor in the world. It wraps 90 feet around the Conde Nast building, reaches 8 stories high, and cost $37 million to construct and maintain.

Though the 10,000-square-foot display is interrupted by a grid of office windows, you wouldn't know that standing in the street. The monitor itself appears seamless. Its 8,200 panels, each 18 inches thick, are affixed to a curved frame. The result is 8 simultaneously operated screens displaying text and video on what amounts to 18 million light-emitting diodes, or LEDs—you know, the little lights on your stereo's VU meter and those that make up the ubiquitous "talking radio" display signs in banks, supermarkets, or wherever you are required to stand in line. If the NASDAQ Tower is any indication, there's work aplenty for multimedia designers, no doubt about it.

ENABLED BY TECHNOLOGY

Just what is multimedia, and what does it take to work in this industry?

Technically, multimedia is simply a product that combines more than one form of media—video, audio, and text. For that reason, many in the industry prefer the terms *new media*, *interactive media*, or *digital media*.

Basically, the interactive digital media industry is a creative industry that is enabled rather than driven by technology, according to a multimedia report. The common elements of the products created is their nonlinear nature; that is, users have the opportunity of accessing information or entering different "worlds" in a game, in any order, at any pace they choose. This interactivity allows digital media to be utilized in numerous products and services that address various business and consumer needs.

UNIQUE CULTURE

A rather unique culture exists in the multimedia industry. It is characterized by the following:

- Most office environments are extremely casual and conducive to a creative team effort.

- Many people prefer the freedom and flexibility of a freelance career path over the security and benefits of employee status.

- Long hours for both employees and contractors are routine, and deadline pressures often dictate marathon sessions.

- An entrepreneurial business spirit exists among employees in many companies, where stock options and profit sharing are common.

So what must you do to enter and succeed in multimedia?

The number one competency expressed by industry is the ability to work in a group. This is an industry where virtually all products are produced by teams. The seamless merger between the artist and the technological elements of a project requires cooperation from all team members. The popularity of the studio model often means teams are made up of members who may not have previously worked together. Therefore, the ability to work effectively with others is key.

Here's a web posting for the job of Interactive Media Designer and Flash Expert. Do you fit in? Is this you a few years from now?

We guarantee this position offers more artistic license and opportunity for creative expression than any other advertised interactive media design position available in the entire country!

Responsibilities:

- Work closely with our studio's directors and design team to create interactive experiences for the Web and other electronic media.

- Provide leadership and expertise in concept development, original art creation, site design/development, and QA.

- Develop innovative Flash animations, navigation systems, interface designs, site architecture, and illustrations.

- Push the state-of-the-art with every creation and thrive in our small, fast-paced, award-winning studio.

The ad goes on to list **Skills and Characteristics**. Here are just a few:

- Must be widely creative and obsessively meticulous.

- Knowledge of Flash as if your career depended on it.

- Exceptional design talents, stylistic breadth, and a demonstrated interest and passion for pushing the limits of the media.

- Sense of humor and perspective, self-motivated, good communicator, comfortable following directions, and able to balance great design with meeting short deadlines.

- Minimum two years' experience as an interactive media designer. Bachelor's degree in Fine Arts, Graphic Design, or related design discipline is a plus, but not required.

Multimedia! Obviously the career requires multiple abilities.

THE DIGITAL DIVIDE

Web site design, photography, multimedia, and even packaging design—it's all digital or going digital. There are careers here for graphic designers that simply didn't exist a decade ago. Such designers are in a position to reap the rewards. Just be sure you stay on the right side of the digital divide.

COMPANIES THAT ARE DOING IT

Here is a short list of art and graphic design companies advertising their services on the Internet:

3-D Central

http://www.3dcentral.com/

Offers 3-D character and technical animation for video, CD-ROM, and web development.

3-dd Digital Design

http://www.3dd.com/

Offers Digital Asset Management, digital photography, 3-D modeling, animation, and multimedia design and production.

Active

http://www.activeinc.com/

Graphic design for Intranet and web solutions, traditional media, and interactive multimedia. Features examples of work and contact details.

Bent Media

http://www.bentmedia.com/

Develops interactive media for clients in higher education, the arts, and the corporate world.

BW Design

http://www.nashville.net/~bwdesign/

Specializes in custom-designed logo work, digital illustrations, and photo manipulation.

People
Who Are Doing It

MEET MIKE LEJEUNE

VITAL STATISTICS

Mike is no longer on the board or in front of his computer screen on a day-to-day basis; being project manager at KBDA, he simply doesn't have time. But he has been there, for sure. With a long history of design work, art direction, and writing, Mike is a designer's designer in many ways. His perspective on the entire field, not just web site design, is important.

❏ PRESENT JOB

Project Manager, KBDA.

❏ KEEPING THE OVERHEAD LOW

"While we have only 12 full-time employees, given the work coming our way, we could hire a few more, no doubt about it," says Mike. "But throughout our 18 years, we have always chosen to grow slowly. We are big enough to handle almost any assignment, yet small enough to pick and choose, say yes or no to what we like and dislike. Because we are not struggling to meet a huge payroll, we don't have to take on jobs we would prefer not to do."

❏ WEB BASICS

"Web design came to us through annual reports," Mike says. "Clients simply began asking us to translate what we were doing with their reports into a web environment. Of course, it wasn't that simple—designing for the Web has its own requirements."

Mike has some strong thoughts on what makes a good web site designer. "We would not hire someone who has done nothing but web sites," he says. "We want a person who grew into that environment. We think of it this way: 'If you have a solid background in design principles, you can be successful in web design.' Learning the new technology is the easy part. When we hire someone, we'll teach them. And in the process, we'll all learn together."

MEET KATHRYN RUSSELL

VITAL STATISTICS

Kathryn, owner of her own studio, is a food photographer. Her clients include Nestlé, Target, Disney, and Ralph's Market, just to name four. Her style shows itself in the warm, diffused light you see in her food images.

❏ PRESENT JOB

Photographer and owner of Kathryn Russell Studios.

❏ GETTING ONE INCREDIBLE PICTURE

"It looks good enough to drink—almost," Kathryn enthuses. The problem, though, is the chocolate milkshake has begun to settle in its traditional soda fountain glass. After all, the concoction's been sitting atop a meticulously creased tablecloth for three hours. It has taken that long for Kathryn just to get the lighting right: adjusting soft boxes, umbrellas, and grid spots.

Now, with her $3,400 large-format camera secured on an even more expensive monopod (single-legged camera support), Kathryn is ready to replace the stand-in milkshake with a fresh, mouth-watering treat. "I'll mix the new beverage myself," she says. "Then I'll snap a dozen photographs in the hope of getting one incredible picture."

❏ STOCK SHOCK

Kathryn, like all professional photographers, is hearing not only the footsteps of 1's and 0's, the march to digital technology, but another (some would say) more evil encroachment. Stock photography houses, those that make available royalty and royalty-free images, are exploding and thus impacting the work of photographers looking for assignments. Kathryn has felt the pinch. "Take, as an example, a grocery store account," she says. "Every week they would send out a mailer with my shots of broccoli, lettuce, tomatoes. Now, someone supplies royalty-free CDs that a client can use over and over again. All of a sudden, that portion of my photography is gone."

"The stock photography issue affects all in the business," Kathryn continues. "Take an annual report. The picture of a guy sitting at his desk on the phone is probably from a stock agency. Time was they would hire a photographer to shoot it. Sure, someone, presumably a professional photographer, snapped the original photograph. Still, stock photos have impacted the photographer and the amount of work she can get."

MEET STEVEN SIKORA

VITAL STATISTICS

Steve, along with his wife, is a partner in Design Guys, which (despite its name) employs mostly women designers. For many years he worked for nonprofits, following his heart so to speak. Steve now does the same with Design Guys, where business is so good they recently added eight additional workstations.

❏ PRESENT JOB

Chief package designer.

❏ SCREAMING BULLET POINTS

"There is so much noise in the mass-market environment," says Steve, "you've got to keep your packaging design simple. Many feel a good package has to have 16 photos on it, screaming bullet points, arrows, and **As Seen on TV** to draw attention. Actually, with all the visual competition out there, if you do something simple and quiet you'll get more attention."

Steve, too, likes the long shelf life aspect to packaging design. "A lot of what we do as graphic designers," he says, "is fleeting: a direct mail piece that goes out once and an ad format that appears a couple of times. Packaging has to be around for awhile; it has to withstand a lot of scrutiny. The other stuff is a bit more for the moment."

❏ FRONTING FOR MICHAEL GRAVES

Recently, when the Target department store chain sought to distinguish itself from other mass-market retailers, it brought in famed international graphic designer Michael Graves to design a new line of kitchenware products specifically for them. Design Guys, from the beginning, designed the packaging for Graves' pots and pans.

According to *Time Magazine*, the new Michael Graves appliances, from a toaster to an ice bucket, have altered Target's image forever. Great packaging for the products had a lot to do with that.

MEET BRENT MCMAHAN

VITAL STATISTICS

When Brent attended college back in 1984, there wasn't much going on in multimedia so he went out and started his own company. "Actually," he says, "in the following ten years I started a lot of companies. That was the nature of what was going on at the time. It has taken me awhile to find a niche."

❏ PRESENT JOB

Vice president, Interactive Media, Sibley Peteet Design.

❏ JACK-OF-ALL-TRADES

"I head up all the interactive stuff," says Brent of his current position at Sibley Peteet Design. "Anything not in print I am in charge of. If it winds up on a computer screen, I probably had something to do with it."

What makes for a good multimedia person today might surprise you. According to Brent, "It isn't just knowing about the hottest software packages. We need folks familiar with movement, dance, chirography. New media are moving to more lifelike actions. We must have people who understand facial expressions, what happens when someone turns her head. People who know how people move will be in high demand."

❏ DON'T HARD WIRE ANYTHING

Brent cautions all who are still in school to be open to everything. "I wouldn't hard wire anything, with regard to new technology and software," he cautions. "By the time you graduate, it will all be different."

A FEW KEY POINTS TO REMEMBER

- The need for those who can do good web design has never been greater.
- Even if you don't plan to specialize in web design, plan to find out all you can about it.
- Digital photography is revolutionizing the role of the professional photographer.
- Digital photography is resulting in the merging of traditional roles compared with the graphic designer.
- A good package designer never forgets that the ultimate purpose is to sell a product.
- With packaging design, keeping it simple is often the best policy.
- Multimedia is a highly collaborative effort.
- Multimedia is enabled, rather than driven, by technology.

CHAPTER SIX

Product Designers

"**O**ur job is to bridge the gap between what marketing wants to sell and what the customer wants to buy," says Eric Ostendorff of Mattel's Hot Wheels design group. "You must be a jack-of-all-trades and not just with your hands. Do you understand costing, safety, marketability, advertisability, and playability? As toy designers, we wear many hats."

"Demand for interior designers has never been better," according to Mayer Rus, editor-in-chief of *Interior Design.* "All firms—small, medium, and large—are desperate for competent staff. Poaching is even going on. Design firms are raiding each other."

Product designers work in a three-dimensional world. As such, they combine technical knowledge of methods, materials, and tools with design talent to create and improve the appearance and function of everything from jewelry to building interiors. Design ability, precision draftsmanship, model-building skill, and a knowledge of type, form, and color are required.

In this chapter we look at four careers incorporating art and craft.

- The jewelry designer must know jewels and how to mount them using a wide range of materials to form an esthetic whole that is also mechanically and technically functional. In addition to the esthetic, a knowledge of strengths and materials is important. One must know how to engineer the piece.

- A toy designer has to possess mechanical skills and a love of gadgetry in addition to an artistic playfulness. Knowing something about electronics would also be helpful. About 60 percent of all new toys come with a computer chip inside.

- The display artist and exhibit designer create a story in space. Such individuals are skilled in composition and visual framing, model making, and the use of diagrams, graphics, and working drawings.

- Interior designers go into an empty room and figure out how to fill the space. They prepare plans like those drawn by an architect, make sketches on a pad or on a laptop, and may even build fully furnished interior scale models.

So let's proceed—let's see what it means to work in three dimensions.

JEWELRY DESIGN: ART IN MINIATURE

Geometric patterns, modular systems, and two or more parts working together as one whole are concepts that motivate Kathleen DiResta of Kathleen DiResta Design. They influence her as a jewelry designer. With precious metals and stones as her vehicle, she creates pieces of jewelry that are not only visually rhythmical but also act as playful objects of art. Interlocking stones and shapes, moveable parts, and unique connections allow the wearer of her art to interact with the pieces. These sculptures, in miniature, invite people who enjoy wearing everyday jewelry to play, smile, and keep a light heart.

If your artistic flair tends toward the miniature, the intricate, the precise, and the elegant, jewelry design is a career to consider. After all, there are currently about 15,000 openings—nationwide—for bench jewelers, the skilled workers who can design and ply metal, set and polish precious stones, and repair finished jewelry. A once private, ethnically dominated, insular industry is seeking designers anywhere it can find them.

MAKING IT BEAUTIFUL

A few such designers do nothing but design; that is, they draw the pieces, by hand or on a computer, to be sculpted by others. Model makers, on the other hand, build the prototypes or one-of-a-kind pieces they design themselves or that were designed by others. And, of course, there are those in the jewelry trade who size and repair pieces as well as mass-produce them.

If you're employed in the jewelry business, you may work in house, for such places as Tiffany's and Cartier, or for large manufacturers who in turn sell to major outlets such as Saks Fifth Avenue and Macy's. Or you could work freelance and perhaps develop your own line of jewelry to be sold in galleries, at trade shows, in small, medium, and large retail outlets, or over the Internet. Finally, you might do strictly custom work for a select clientele.

Regardless of what facet of jewelry design you engage in, being able to craft a beautiful piece or at least know how it is done, is vital. According to Claudia Endler, whose clean, elegant, modern-looking designs are widely received, there are essentially two ways to produce a piece of jewelry:

"One is the fabrication method, where you actually work in the metal itself," she says. "You hammer it, shape it, form it, and cut it. Or you can assemble it; that is, manufacture the object yourself using wire. Either way, the process involves bending, forming, and shaping metal, usually by adding heat.

"Then we have the lost wax process, where a refractory mold is built up around a sculpted wax piece. The mold, with the wax inside, is baked so as to melt and drain off the wax. Metal is now poured into the cavity, the mold is broken, and the rough metal piece removed, to be refined with precision tools."

3-D IN MINIATURE

What Gretchen Frutz, a longtime jewelry designer, loves about the process is its three-dimensional aspect. "In jewelry design, you must be careful," she cautions. "Can the piece you are drawing actually be made? In many respects, it's an engineering problem, similar to the construction of any project, whether it is an automobile or an office building. A lot of things you draw cannot be made in three dimensions; strength and materials have to be considered. I have been doing this for more than 20 years. Every new piece is not only an artistic challenge, it's an engineering problem."

What skills does one need to work in jewelry? What makes a good jewelry designer and crafter?

"I can pick up a cigarette ash without breaking it," says Gretchen. "When I paint, it is with a single hair, almost. It is sculpting in miniature, the tiniest scale possible. Even one-tenth of a millimeter can make a difference when you are looking at a face only three millimeters tall."

So, where to gain the knowledge, where to acquire the skills?

"I have an associate degree in jewelry design from the Fashion Institute of Technology (FIT) in New York," says Stephanie Occhipinti, president of the Jewelry Design Professionals' Network (JDPN). "But you can't learn everything in school. It can give you only the bits and pieces, then experience takes over."

Claudia at first felt intimidated, not having a degree in jewelry design or a certificate from GIA, the Gemological Institute of America. Then she discovered places where she could take classes, from night schools to university extension programs to art schools.

From then on, Claudia worked in the business, learning the do's and don'ts, the cans and cannots—that, and developing her own style. Claudia has come to find jewelry design a wonderful form of artistic expression, one, fortunately, people are willing to pay her to voice.

TOY STORY

Caleb and Christi Chung, a husband-and-wife toy design team, had just returned from their annual trek to Toy Fair, the largest toy trade show in the Western Hemisphere, held in New York City every February.

"Once again we were underwhelmed," Caleb, a former Hollywood special effects developer, says. "We determined then and there to stop working altogether, return home to Boise, Idaho, and take the plunge, spending the next six months creating a product we knew our background and knowledge would allow us to perfect and exploit."

Toiling in their garage, the Chungs conjured up a being destined for life.

"I wanted to make it small and inexpensive," Caleb explains. "I started with a 3-inch-high cone. We added a nose, a mouth, eyes, ears, and feet. We gave it a tilt and a bit of movement, and we crammed it full of gears and electronics, the latter developed by our new partner, David Hamton.

"Christi did the drawings, taking ideas from owls, hamsters, and the like. But in the end, we purposely developed a critter like no other, a three-dimensional being with emotions. Kids could invest hours in making the furry friend anything they wanted it to be."

Next, the Chungs produced a video—a commercial, if you will—and took it to the toy companies. "We didn't go to Mattel or Hasbro, the big guys," says Caleb. "With only 13 weeks left to the next Toy Fair, time was running out. Tiger Electronics, a company light on its feet, was our choice. They bought it on the condition that David, Christi, and I would work for them to see the product through, bring it to life."

And to life it came!

With, at its peak, $1\frac{1}{2}$ to 2 million tiny creatures named Furby selling every month, the Chungs brainchild has become possibly the most successful toy ever made. "You hope for a big hit," says Caleb. "Then you hope for longevity. Only time will tell."

PRODUCT DESIGN FOR THE KID IN US

Toy design, perhaps the ultimate product design for the kid in all of us, is a booming area within this design field. According to the Toy Manufacturers of America, Inc. (TMA), total industry sales for 1998 hit $27.2 billion. That's a 20 percent increase over 1996 if you don't include video games, and a 10 percent increase if you do.

But what makes a good toy designer? Isn't such a person more an engineer than a graphic artist? "The best designers," David Voss, design manager for the Nurf and Vehicles division of Hasbro Corporation in Cincinnati, Ohio, explains, "are those who understand three key areas: design, engineering, and marketing. Often, we get new hires who are completely focused on design. Not good! You have to ask, 'How are you going to market the toy? How are you going to make the darn thing?'"

Yet, the kid thing is for real, too. In this business, you must always ask, "Is this something a child is going to pick up and play with?" Clearly, you must understand how children think and act, what they want.

However, appealing to kids and their wants is not enough. Any product, including a toy, has to be made and sold. Adults are involved.

Elliot Rudell, founder of Rudell Design, a new product development and invention company and a respected inventor in the field, puts it this way: "A guy will come to me and say, 'I have a great idea for a toy, kids will love it.' My face does not move. In the real world, I too have to love it, the guy at the conference table has to love it, his company has to love it, and the buyer has to love it, thinking it will sell to the kids, and, equally important, to their parents. As a toy designer, you're in a creative field, but if you are going to be commercially creative, that puts restrictions on you. Can you live with those limitations? If not, do something else."

TOY COLLEGE

So, where to get training, where to study toy design?

On the fifth floor of Otis College of Art and Design, Gabriel Delatorre is carving a 4-inch piece of wood into a VW Bug. "I'll vacuum-form it with styrene later, then paint and detail the mold," the nineteen-year-old junior explains. "I'm learning to execute a prototype model."

Gabriel is a full-time student at one of only a handful of "toy colleges" in the United States, the other notable one being FIT, the same school Stephanie, our jewelry designer, attended.

When Gabriel completes his studies, he'll have earned a Bachelor of Fine Arts in toy design. Otis, which has a distinguished reputation in the fine arts field, began offering toy studies in 1997. Their first graduating class was in June 2000. "Our program trains students in developing soft and hard toys,

Chair Martin Caveza says. "Of course, we also cover safety issues, game theory, child psychology, and business practices."

To be sure, you do not have to attend a big-name toy college to make it as a toy designer. Obviously the majority of those doing such design did not attend Otis or FIT "There are many routes to designing the next Furby," says Caleb. "First go to a place like Otis or on-the-job training at Mattel. Next, buy a ticket, hop on a plane, and get to the Toy Fair in New York every February. Then haunt your local Toys Я Us. You must know everything that's in the store and why it's changing. Make the place your research facility."

EXHIBIT DESIGNERS

E-3, 2000, the Electronic Entertainment Expo, held at the Los Angeles Convention Center in May 2000, was a multimedia extravaganza. Nowhere was this more apparent than at the room-sized exhibit housing MPLAYER.COM, the premier on-line multiplayer gaming service. And, if the multimedia electronic action didn't grab your attention, the exhibit itself was sure to. Here was a mega multimedia presentation all its own. The exhibit, costing tens of thousands of dollars to design, fabricate, and install, occupied 1,000 square feet on three raised floors, where fanatic gamers battled it out on a dozen big-screen overhead monitors.

In-line, peninsula, and island exhibit configurations, with curved frames, flat frames, bridges, and headers, were everywhere. The design and construction represented an engineering marvel. Trade zone truss-and-counter systems, and legend, pop-up, and channel-panel displays interlocked within the arena. But more than being structurally sound, the edifice was visually striking. The work of graphic designers, with its dazzling colored images, attention-getting animations, and pulsing lights, was in evidence throughout. Nothing had been left to chance in the exhibit's design. Traffic flow was optimized for gamers (young and old), and "suits," who were looking to make deals, were cocooned in soundproof glass enclosures hugging the perimeter. Art, structural design, and ergonomics had come together to create a wonder in itself.

LEMONADE STAND FOR GROWNUPS

Designing such trade-show exhibits, the grownup equivalent of a lemonade stand, is big business: despite (or perhaps because of) the explosion in cyber relationships, face-to-face business dealings are more important than ever.

In 1999 there were 4,053 commercial exhibitions held in the United States in 514 million net square feet of exhibit space. In all, 123 million people attended trade shows.

Interior exhibit design, a subcategory of environmental graphic design, finds application beyond trade shows, of course. There's permanent installation work in natural history and art museums, science and technology exhibition centers, and travel and tourism information venues. And don't forget all those retail stores and shopping malls. It seems exhibit designers are displaying their work everywhere.

But how do artists and graphic designers fit into this picture? What are their roles?

According to Norm Friedrich, president of Octanorm, an exhibition-stand construction and retail display equipment company with offices in Toronto and Atlanta, "There's plenty of work for designers who can provide a structural and decorative framework on which to hold substrates and graphics. The key is in understanding modularity, what it takes to assemble and disassemble the items multiple times. It's like messing with Tinkertoys."

DESIGN PLUS CRAFT

Those who work well in this field combine a graphic design sense with craft skills. "What makes me qualified as an exhibit designer," says Joe Steiner of Custom Exhibits Corporation in Broken Arrow, Oklahoma, "is that I have actually built the stuff. You must be able to make it in three dimensions. Can you unfold those shapes and puzzles in your head? Do you have a concept of materials and structures?"

Those who usually wind up designing exhibits have a background in industrial or even theatrical design. They don't need an engineering degree, but actual construction or cabinetmaking experience would be a big help.

Some sales and marketing experience would also be a plus. Why? Because as a trade show exhibit designer you must never forget your purpose: to design a booth that will facilitate the sales of products and services offered.

For example, if you are going to consider the exhibit a marketing tool and not a form of artistic expression, a person should be able to walk down the aisle at a crowded show and discover there is something about your booth that, at a minimum, keeps it from being unnoticed. The potential customer has to at least see it. An attendee must be able to glance at the booth and tell instantly who you are and what you're selling.

You must ask: "Do these people in the booth look like someone I want to do business with? Are they organized, attentive, and under control in a professional environment?"

Achieving all this has as much to do with understanding traffic flow as it does with good exhibit design. "If you have a large booth but bad traffic flow, everything gets jammed up," says Joe. "You defeat your purpose."

The bottom line? You're trying to create a selling environment. There was a time when designers and artists struggled with exhibit design because they where concentrating on something that was aesthetically pleasing. Yes, it attracted attention and looked nice, but often, the salespeople trying to sell out of such an environment went crazy. "The key is to create an environment a person can work out of, present product out of, welcome guests into," explains Joe. "If someone in the aisle stands back and looks up in awe at a booth, great. But if he then walks on, the design is a failure."

WALK-THROUGH ON THE LAPTOP

To get there—to a great exhibit design—the latest in computer technology is (as in most design work today) fully employed. "There was a time," Joe says, "when I would pound two nails into a drawing board to set up my perspective points, then proceed with my presentation rendering. Now I use DENEBA-CAD, with which I can build virtual models, adjust the lighting, and create a walk-through path for the potential customer. I then send my salesperson out with a laptop that is plopped down on the client's desk. With the twirl of a pointer, the virtual model spins around. It is a great marketing and design tool."

"We are also doing animated walk-throughs," adds Norm. "The client views the exhibit before it's ever built."

So, what does it take to design in this exciting, creative, and growing aspect of art and graphic design?

"Adding a third dimension is like adding another multiplier to the formula," says Joe. "It makes it algebra instead of arithmetic. Can you fold it down and put it in a cigar case, then when it springs open, can you put your car under it? That's what the customer wants."

While the creative graphic design element is certainly needed, in this industry you must include some sort of technical skill. It goes beyond the artistry. You have to create things that are realistic to build.

INTERIOR DESIGNER

"The public thinks we do nothing but pick colors and fluff pillows," Doug Stead, executive vice president of the California Council of Interior Design Certification, says. "It doesn't understand that hotels or restaurants have been designed by an interior designer."

BEYOND DECORATING

Interior designers, approximately 55,000 nationwide, analyze a client's needs, goals, and safety requirements; develop design concepts that are appropriate, functional, and pleasing to the eye; select materials, finishes, furnishings, fixtures, and equipment; prepare working drawings and specifications for non-load-bearing interior construction; and administer bids and contract documents as the client's agent. They specialize in such areas as homes, offices, shopping malls, hospitals, hotels, restaurants, childcare centers, museums, theaters, schools, industrial facilities, and even set design. Their purpose is not only to make interiors look better (the status-based approach) but to make them more functional (the task-based approach). Clearly, this is a field within art and graphic design that is more than hanging draperies and choosing wallpaper.

Many interior designers find employment in design firms—small, medium, and large. Such firms, according to *Interior Design Magazine*, specialize in offices (51 percent); hotels and restaurants (11 percent); medical facilities (8 percent); and residential (4 percent). While the latter is only a tiny percentage of the design firm business, home interiors is where the majority of single-proprietor interior designers work. According to Jerry Harke, marketing manager for the American Society of Interior Designers (ASID), "More than 70 percent of our 20,000 professional designers own or manage their design firms."

INTENSELY PERSONAL

Many paths exist to becoming educated and trained in interior design. Certificate and two-year and four-year programs abound. You must be sure, however, to select an accredited program, one recognized by the Foundation for Interior Design Education Research (FIDER) or the National Association of Schools of Art and Design (NASAD), to name two certifying bodies.

One such program, accredited by FIDER, is the UCLA Extension Professional Designation in Interior Design. It is an example of the rigor required to succeed as an interior design student.

At UCLA, you take a 38-course sequence that instills equal parts practical theory and creative training. According to the Extension catalog:

Traditional skills and artistry are taught alongside new technologies and an awareness of emerging socioeconomic and environmental issues. Curriculum areas include history, theory, and culture; design communications, including drawing, drafting, and CAD; space planning, construction details, and lighting; and professional practices, research, and career preparation.

In addition, many state and national organizations provide certification in the interior design field. The National Council for Interior Design Certification (NCIDQ) is one such association. You don't need to be certified by NCIDQ or any other organization to practice as an interior designer, but after passing the NCIDQ exam and meeting specific experience qualifications, you may call yourself a Certified Interior Designer (CID)—a big plus.

Regardless of how you are educated, trained, or certified in interior design, it is important to keep in mind the people aspects of the business. "It's intensely personal," says Desi Kovacs, Interior Design Department Chair, Learning Tree University (LTU) in Chatsworth, California. "You are bringing to your clients some level of ability to tell them how to live their lives. You must help them create *their* vision, not your own."

"Designer/client relations—that's what it's all about," says Nicki Jackson of Nicki J. Interiors. "Are you someone the clients can trust, someone they want in their home? After all, the clients often give you a key to their house; you're in there when they're not. You're working with their money."

As with exhibit design, those with an art and graphic design sense who wish to work in a three-dimensional world where a built environment is an integral part of the picture will find interior design an excellent art-based choice.

TAKING SHAPE IN THREE DIMENSIONS

Whether you're working as a jewelry, toy, exhibit, or interior designer, you are putting together pieces in a three-dimensional world. To be sure, these four fields are only representative—not inclusive—of product design as a whole. There's the broad field of industrial design with its emphasis on things mechanical. Furniture designers work in a built environment all their own. And those designing everything from a new line of stylish staplers to desk lamps and refrigerators are to be included. If what you want to do is to take shape in three dimensions, welcome to the world of product design.

COMPANIES THAT ARE DOING IT

Here are a few companies specializing in product design:

3-D Environments
http://www.geocities.com/tokyo/towers/5051/
New York designer Graig Meachen produces 2-D and 3-D backgrounds, virtual reality worlds, and web development. He offers animated fly-throughs of work.

A Brothers & Associates
http://www.abrothers.com/java/index-j.htm
The fact sheet on the design group comprises exhibit designers, graphic designers, and interior design specialists. Includes photo examples of past work.

Advanced Media Design
http://www.amdrendering.com/
Creates graphical renderings of architectural designs. Picture portfolio plus QuickTime or RealSpace VR tour are available.

Architectural Collaborative
http://www.archocollab.com/
Multidiscipline firm that offers architectural, trade-show exhibit, and presentation design.

ArtDept USA, The
http://www.artdeptusa.com/
A vast array of services that includes web site design, graphic design, photography, and retail signage.

People
Who Are Doing It

MEET KATHLEEN DIRESTA

VITAL STATISTICS

Kathleen, age thirty, a New York City resident, designs and creates her own line of jewelry. She sells her pieces in about thirty galleries across the country and in Japan. She recently opened her own gallery, Kathleen DiResta Design, which features jewelry, furniture, sculpture, and eclectic housewares, all made by Kathleen and her artistic brothers, one of whom is a toy designer.

❏ PRESENT JOB

Owner, Kathleen DiResta Design.

❏ A LONG ROAD TO SUCCESS

Kathleen's route to acceptance as a jewelry designer is instructive. In its plot, it shows a willingness—a necessity—to learn all aspects of the business, to immerse oneself in every aspect, to gain experience any way one can.

"When I was in college," she says, "I studied sculpture. While working my way through school, I took a summer job at a jewelry store in New York City.

It was production work, in sterling silver only. I didn't do any soldering; I only finished the pieces, polished them, set the stones. Then the owner would send me out to buy supplies. Although I didn't realize it at the time, I was making valuable contacts: where to buy gems and other materials. Then he sent me to trade and craft shows. All the while, I was learning the business."

After graduating from college in 1994, Kathleen walked into another jewelry store ready to work full time. "The woman running the business needed an assistant, and I was it," she says. "She taught me how to work in 18- and 22-karat gold, how to solder, how to do granulations, the ancient technique of fusing little balls and wires to the surface to create ornate—almost museum—pieces. I was traveling everywhere, picking it all up. It was like a modern-day apprenticeship."

After three intensive workshops at the Rivera Academy of Jewelry Arts in San Francisco, followed by 12-hour days at a production house in New York, Kathleen was ready to go out on her own. "After working that hard," she says, "I figured it was better to do it for myself."

❑ SUCCESS EQUALS PLAIN, HARD WORK

What does it take to succeed? "Lots of hard work, commitment, dedication, enthusiasm, and confidence," says Kathleen. "You must find a way to keep your mental peace amid the craziness of running your own business."

MEET ERIC OSTENDORFF

VITAL STATISTICS

Eric, thirty-eight, with sixteen years in toy design, has always been a practical, hands-on, mechanically oriented guy. Growing up in Virginia and going to college there, he took advantage of all the interning and co-op programs available. "Few in this field are degreed engineers," he says. "Most, perhaps 80 percent, have a practical crafts background. Many are graphic design graduates."

❏ PRESENT JOB

Toy designer in Mattel's Hot Wheels Division, specializing in track layouts.

❏ KID APPRECIATION

Knowing what kids want, really want, is still the bottom line in toy design. It is not always the latest, greatest stuff. "I'll give you an example," Eric says. "If I could get a toy car to levitate, float in the air, that would be a major technological achievement. But only an adult could appreciate the feat. Test that technology against a set where the car does a simple loop and smashes into other cars, and a kid will opt for the latter every time."

❏ ADULT PURCHASES

"People say, 'I can think of a great toy, I watched my kids play, I know what they want,'" Eric says. "At any party I meet ten of those folks, but what I don't meet is the person who says, 'You know, I just made this really cool thing that does this and that.' It's that practicality again, the ability to sort out the problems, make something that is cost-effective, something people—particularly parents—would be interested in buying. It's where the rubber meets the road, if you'll excuse the pun."

MEET KEN BELL

VITAL STATISTICS ━━━━━━━━━

Ken, twenty-eight, owner of Trade Show Direct, started out with trade show graphics only, but he got tired of doing just the graphics; he wanted to design, build, and sell the booths as well. Today, with Trade Show Direct, he is a one-stop shop employing five people: artists, designers, and crafters specializing in trade-show displays and large-format digital graphics.

❏ PRESENT JOB

Owner of Trade Show Direct.

❏ BIG IS BEAUTIFUL

"The big difference with exhibit designers has to do with size," Ken says. "Take the graphics placed onto the display itself. Most graphic designers are used to working with $8^1/_2$ by 11 inches. With us it is more like $8^1/_2$ by 11 feet, actually 8 by 10. A file resolution for the former would take up perhaps 30 megabytes. For the latter, make that 200 megabytes."

❏ COMPUTER KNOW-HOW—GET IT ANY WAY YOU CAN

"You are simply unemployable without them," says Ken, referring to computer skills. "You certainly don't need a four-year degree to work here, but you must know the software. I have no problem with hiring two-year graduates, or even those who did their training in one year. In the end, it all comes down to taking several classes to get your feet wet, then having the motivation to learn the rest on your own. No matter how, school or self-taught, you're going to spend lots of time learning the software."

MEET NICKI JACKSON

VITAL STATISTICS

Nicki Jackson, forty something, is proprietor of Nicki J. Interiors. She's been in the business for twelve years. "I had hit my mid-thirties and needed a career to fall back on," she explains. "I enrolled at Learning Tree University (LTU) and the rest is history, as they say."

❏ PRESENT JOB

Proprietor of her own interior design business, Nicki J. Interiors.

❏ PAYING HER DUES

"My first job was in sales, selling interiors at a furniture store in a local mall," Nicki confides, in discussing her start. "Soon after, I asked my boss if he thought of offering an interior design service. I had my certificate from LTU and I wanted to apply what I knew. I spent the next year as their interior designer on call."

Nicki's first assignment as an independent interior designer, someone working for herself, was an eye-opener. "A contractor had a sister who had just died," she explains. "The contractor, a woman, was still in mourning. I was asked to accompany her to the sister's house and make any suggestions for changes. When I offered my opinion, the contractor said, 'Why that's just what my sister would have wanted. I want to hire you.' I said, 'You do?' I wanted to stuff those words right back in my mouth. I was trying to act so cool and professional."

❏ THE TALENT MUST SHOW

Nicki has come a long way since those early, struggling years when she was so surprised that anyone wanted her services. Speaking of her profession in general, she says, "The right training and education are important. Knowing how to run a business is essential, but in the end, it's about ability. Do you have a flair—even love—for interior design? You must make clients feel your passion—and then absorb it."

A FEW KEY POINTS TO REMEMBER

- Jewelry designers need to know how their product is engineered.
- Jewelry is made by metal fabrication or the lost wax process.
- There are numerous jewelry design classes available at all levels of study.
- Toys must have kid appeal, but they are usually purchased by adults.
- The best toy designers are those who understand three key areas: design, engineering, and marketing.
- Toy designer wannabes should visit Toy Fair, held in New York City every February.
- Trade shows are a $100-billion-a-year business.
- Exhibit designers must know how to construct the product.
- Exhibit designers need to consider their exhibit as a marketing tool for the client, not a vehicle for self-expression.
- Interior designers do more than pick colors and fluff pillows.
- Only 4 percent of all interior designers work in residential environments.
- Certification is a real plus for an interior designer.

CHAPTER SEVEN

Interning in the Arts

"I wasn't sure I wanted to work here, at Intervisual Books, when my professor first suggested I apply for an internship," says Salina Yoon, now an art director at the company. "Yes, I longed to do children's book illustrations. But Intervisual, the world leader in pop-up books, sent most illustration work out to freelancers. Nonetheless, I signed on. Not only did I get to illustrate, I wound up designing as well. But my interning experience was short-lived. Three weeks after it began, they hired me full time."

Whether you eventually seek employment in an in-house corporate design department, an advertising agency, a design firm, or self-employment as a freelancer, as a student in art or graphic design, you're almost certain to begin work while still in school, as an intern. Virtually required for all creative types, it's best to plan early in your educational experience for what is usually a non-paid, yet invaluable on-the-job work experience. We begin in this chapter by examining interning and what you can expect to gain from the on-site adventure.

We then take up the résumé. We discuss the basics, as well as what it takes to construct, in this digital age, a computer-friendly document.

In art and graphic design, the portfolio is key, your talent indicator. We explore what must be included, as well as some valuable portfolio do's and don'ts.

The information interview is a great way to investigate a possible internship experience and also gain a broader understanding of a firm's operation. We show you how to succeed with this role-reversal interview.

Finally, getting out and about and attending art and graphic design-related conferences can open your eyes as well as company doors. As a logical extension of your interning experience, we supply tips on how to maximize the effectiveness of your visits.

INTERNING: ALL BUT REQUIRED

Interning is hot, the on-campus job-search strategy for the new millennium. More than one-third of all students do internships before graduating. Furthermore, in the visual arts and graphic design, it is all but mandatory; you really shouldn't leave school without it.

For employers, interns represent a threefold benefit.

1. First, such interns become future employees. The employer gets a chance to assess interns' work performance without actually paying them, or at least paying them less than a full-time employee. "I wouldn't have been hired here on the basis of my résumé," says Janet Rey, a graphic design assistant at a leading packaging design firm. "I wouldn't even have made the first cut. Because I was an intern and they knew my work, I got the job."

2. Interns can also mean free labor, a plus for many companies, particularly nonprofit agencies that have been through the 1990s' downsizing binge. As long as employers don't bog down an intern in repetitive, no-brainer, paste-up tasks, there's nothing wrong with

that. It's obvious: If interns are free to move around and do different tasks, enthusiasm and productivity stay up.

3. Many employers view interns as "energy boosters" as well. Bringing new ideas, heightened energy, and real excitement, they pump up the volume by charging everyone up.

Of course, interning can and should be as valuable for the internee as it is for the employer. But to avoid job shock, interns must learn what's expected of them early on. The internship activity should let them experience all aspects of the work environment: the good, the bad, and the boring. That way, they avoid the Catch-22 of "You can't get a job without experience and you can't get experience without a job."

Interns realize employers demand previous training. But with only 100 hours, the intern can then say, "I have work experience." There's also the foot-in-the-door component. Interning can be a ten-week interview for the student. Most employers prefer to hire from within and since interns are already in, they will have the hiring advantage.

In sum, for an internship program to succeed, four elements must be present:

1. The student should do meaningful work, not just hang around looking over the shoulder of an artist or graphic designer.

2. The student shouldn't get stuck in a narrowly defined, repetitive task, where exposure to the occupation and the company is limited.

3. The employer mustn't view the student as free labor to be exploited.

4. The job supervisor should take an active interest in the student's learning on the job.

If these components are met, then an internship program can add considerably to any student's art and graphic design education.

A FIFTY-FIFTY PROPOSITION

Irene Holt is the director of student affairs at Platt College in Cerritos, California. While Platt does not have an internship requirement, all students are encouraged to intern if possible. "We suggest they do it while currently attending classes," Irene says. "That way they have something extra to put on their résumé. In addition, they might end up doing work with an employer that can then be added to their portfolio."

Irene encourages students to begin interning toward the end of their schooling. "I want them to be at least halfway through; that way they have something to offer the employer," she says. "It should be a fifty-fifty proposition; the students get experience, the firm acquires their knowledge, new ideas."

"Also," Irene continues, "students should avoid waiting until after graduation to intern. While still in school, students are in a free-time mode. Once they graduate, they have no time for interning; they have to get to work. I ask students to think of interning as part of their education, as an extra class. That way it's a little easier to fit in."

While interning is a positive, eagerly sought-after experience for most art and graphic design students, it can become exploitative if one isn't careful. Since it is mostly nonpaying and, in many schools, a requirement, the opportunity for employer abuse is obvious. Yet, as Salina at Intervisual Books points out, "It is clearly within our interest here not to have interns filing papers and gophering. When we bring on an intern, we are looking at a future freelancer who, hopefully, will be back working for us in that capacity some day. Therefore, I want to train them now."

It should be that way everywhere.

AVOIDING THE INTERNING NO-NO'S

Okay, you've lined up a design internship at an ad agency, in-house corporate creative department, or design firm, and you're eager to start. But you are also apprehensive. Sure, you have a pretty good idea what must be done to impress and produce. It's what you need to avoid doing that has you worried.

To ease your concern, here are ten no-no's that are most likely to upset any employer (and fellow employees). As an intern, you will want to avoid them at all cost. Doing what's right is important; avoiding what's wrong is critical. According to a national survey, here are the top ten negatives:

1. Dishonesty and lying. It's a new job and, of course, you want to look good, but pumping up your knowledge, experience, and qualifications is one thing; being dishonest or outright lying is quite another.

2. Irresponsibility, goofing off, and attending to personal business on company time. Back in junior high you knew plenty of kids (maybe you were one of them) who let this sort of thing define them. That was then; work is now. Even if you aren't being paid, you are expected to do a job.

3. Arrogance, egotism, and excessive aggressiveness. No matter how well you are doing in school, on any new job you have a lot to learn. Practice a little humility.

4. Absenteeism and tardiness. Over and over again your teachers warned you against coming to class late or not at all. They said such behavior would not be tolerated in the real world, on the job. Guess what? They were right.

5. Not following instructions. Doing it out of ignorance is understandable; after all you are an intern—you'll be cut some slack. Failing to follow instructions on purpose, however, is inexcusable.

6. Ignoring company policies. Company policies aren't created in a day. They develop over months, even years. In many ways such policies define and identify a company. Flagrantly ignoring company policies shows a wanton disregard for the firm's ethos.

7. A whining or complaining attitude toward the company or job. Of course, your internship may not be perfect. There is much about the corporate world that doesn't make sense, is just plain wrong, or is self-serving. But discovering all this is part of your education—why you are interning in the first place.

8. Absence of commitment, concern, or dedication. Even in a hot job market where your skills are in demand, you are lucky to have landed an internship. Act like it.

9. Laziness and a lack of motivation or enthusiasm. See number 8.

10. Taking credit for work done by others. This is a big no-no. Don't hesitate to toot your own horn a bit and sell yourself, even as an intern, but you want to take a tactful, modest approach. Grabbing credit for what others do is like stealing—and that can be the most grievous no-no of all.

Have you had enough of all these negatives? On the positive side, as you begin your internship, be realistic, be patient, be alert, show initiative, be cooperative, be conscientious, be mature, and be inquisitive. If all this sounds a bit like the Boy Scout oath, so be it. Nothing beats a positive attitude.

THE CO-OP OPTION

Closely akin to interning and often confused with it is cooperative (co-op) education. Co-op ed takes internship one step farther—to a paying job. Furthermore, in a co-op program, you're likely to be placed in a clearly defined job category, where you work and earn just the same as everyone else in the company. In co-op programs, the school takes the leading role and the employer is enlisted to "cooperate." The intent is to create a close connection in the student's mind between the job and the classroom. In 1998, 429 two-year colleges placed 81,000 students (77 percent vocational) in co-op programs.

THE RESUME: DOOR OPENER

You can't help but notice; there are books, minicourses, and seminars galore that show you how to prepare a killer résumé, one "guaranteed" to land you a job interview. There's even the National Résumé Writers Association (NRWA). All this résumé interest exists not only because workers are moving from job to job more frequently (on average, once every three years), but because preparing and sending a résumé, thanks to computer résumé-creating programs and the Internet, has never been easier. In fact, many large companies are so inundated with unsolicited résumés they've resorted to employing résumé-scanning software to search for key words in your document.

That aside, there are still basics to keep in mind when preparing a résumé.

1. Your résumé is your personal inventory and formal introduction to a potential employer. Though secondary in importance to your portfolio, it is, nonetheless, a document that must be provided.

2. The résumé's purpose is to get you a job interview—no more, no less. It should stress what you can offer, not what you want; it must state accomplishments, not just descriptions.

3. As a rule, at least with humans involved, résumés are not read, but skimmed; therefore, they should be kept short, preferably one page.

4. Finally, remember the presentation of the résumé: its neatness, the absence of spelling and grammatical errors, and its concise writing style are all as important as the information contained within.

Okay, you say, but what am I going to do if the first one to read my résumé is not a person, but a computer?

That can be a problem. "Everything you used to do five or ten years ago to make your résumé stand out will make it worse today," says Deb Besmer, president and CEO of HireSystems, in Waltham, Massachusetts. "Colored paper, unusual fonts, graphics—all this can mess things up."

Here are some tips to keep in mind when preparing a computer-friendly "vanilla" résumé:

- Avoid unusual type faces, underlining, and italics.

- Use 12- and 14-point type.

- Use smooth white paper, black ink, and quality printing.

- Be sure your name is on the first line of the page.

- Provide white space.

- Avoid double columns.

- Don't fold or staple your résumé. (If mailing, use a large envelope.)

- Use abbreviations carefully.

Some of these points—the avoidance of unusual type faces, the use of white paper only—may be difficult for creative types to adhere to. Keep in mind, again, that the purpose of the résumé is to get you a job interview. Once that's scheduled, you can begin polishing up your portfolio—the one item, more than anything else, that will land you the job.

PORTFOLIO: TALENT INDICATOR

In art and graphic design, talent, more than a résumé or degree, is the basis upon which a hiring decision will be made. And it is the portfolio that is used to judge such talent.

What should a portfolio include? Above all, samples of a candidate's work, rather than long sections of many projects. It should also reflect a variety of styles and exhibit work done in another medium, if necessary, such as painting or sculpture, to showcase talent and skill.

Theo Stephan Williams, in her excellent book *The Streetwise Guide to Freelance Design and Illustration*, 1998, published by North Light Books, an imprint of F&W Publishers, Inc., provides some portfolio do's and don'ts.

Do:

- Make sure you have a new-looking portfolio.

- Clean up your portfolio the day of every review.

- Treat your portfolio like your most prized possession.

- Mount your samples with rubber cement.

- Have at least 12 but no more than 16 samples in your portfolio.

- Place your portfolio on the front- or backseat of your car, not in the trunk where it can slide around.

Don't:

- Leave your portfolio in your car overnight.

- Eat, drink, or let anyone else eat or drink anywhere near your portfolio.

- Skimp on the overall look of your portfolio.

- Check it with your luggage while traveling.

- Let cats, dogs, or other furry animals within 10 feet of your portfolio.

In other words, treat your portfolio with the respect it deserves.

More and more, creative types are developing their own personal web sites, a key purpose of which is to host an on-line portfolio. Not only does such a site make it easier for prospective employers to find your portfolio, but with it the damage issue, a significant problem, becomes moot.

Animation or work with similarly large data files is often presented on a video reel. Keep in mind that short, concise reels are preferred. Companies generally decide within the first minute whether to continue assessing a reel; therefore, it is important to showcase the best work at the start of the reel.

All this portfolio emphasis aside, however, the presentation of your art is not everything—the sole factor that will determine whether you get a job or not. Talent, yes, personality, a double yes. "It is so hard to tell much about artists or graphic designers from their portfolios," says Thomas Rossman, a principal with RLR Advertising and Marketing. "In the end it boils down to personal chemistry, whether they are going to fit in." Worth remembering.

INFORMATION INTERVIEW: SEE AND BE SEEN

If you can't go the full intern route, but you still want to see what's going on in the real world while making valuable industry contacts, why not invite yourself around by setting up an information interview? Such an interview is just what the name indicates—an interview to find out about the job, the company, or the field in general. Remember, people love to talk about their work. Nearly all people, if asked, will give you a 30-minute interview to discuss their favorite subject—themselves, and what they do for a living.

Setting up an information interview can work for you in a number of ways:

1. While you can gain a lot by reading, the most effective way to learn about occupations, jobs within those occupations, and the local job market is through personal contact.

2. Though an information interview is not a job interview, the communications skills and confidence you gain while interviewing someone

for career information will certainly help when it's time for the real thing.

3. Through the information interview, you're likely to meet people who will become valuable job contacts. In many instances, these people will take a direct interest in you and your job search.

4. In the information interview, you are in role reversal, that is, you are the interviewer, not the interviewee.

5. You will quickly learn where the jobs are in your community.

6. The people you interview could eventually steer you to a job opening.

The latter is particularly important. An information interview, if it is to be effective, should be a two-way opportunity. True, you're not seeking a job, just information, but although your purpose is to see, it is also to be seen; while it is to hear, it is also to be heard; while it is to be impressed, it is also to impress; and while it is to find out, it is also to be found out.

In other words, while you want to learn all you can about a company, you want to let them know about you, too. You're on a scouting trip, you're looking for a potential employer, and you're out to make contacts. The information interview is an excellent way to begin.

OUT AND ABOUT: ATTENDING INDUSTRY CONFERENCES

As we discovered in Chapter Six, 123 million people attended industry trade shows in 1999. That number, according to Steve Miller, author of the book *How to Get the Most out of Trade Shows*, represents 85 percent of the working adults in America.

From design conferences sponsored by trade magazines to association extravaganzas, you can find hundreds of places to see the latest advances in art and graphic design, exchange ideas, attend seminars and workshops, and sell yourself. You should consider making attending such conferences a logical extension of your interning experience.

To get the most from these shows, however, you need to go forth with a plan and a purpose. Most conferences are divided into two major components: the exhibitor's section and the technical (breakout) sessions. Entrance into the former is often free; attendance at the latter, however, is usually anything but. Since you are probably a student and likely on a limited budget, let's concentrate on how to get the most from prowling the exhibit area.

In the exhibitor hall, industry representatives set up booths ranging from 60 square feet to footage greater than your house. "It's here where the sights and sounds, the bustle and activity, of the show take place," says Pete Dicks, executive director of the Exhibit Designers and Producers Association (EDPA). "It is a breathtaking place that can be a bit paralyzing, even for seasoned conference goers."

SHOTGUN OR SEARCHLIGHT APPROACH

In exploring the exhibit area, you can take a shotgun or searchlight approach. "If you shotgun it," says Jack Geer, a graphic designer who has attended more than 50 conferences in the last dozen years, "you visit as many exhibits as possible, bag all the literature you can, and usually wind up with sore feet.

"With the searchlight method, you're more focused," he continues. "You visit displays of particular interest, hang around the exhibit, chat at length with company representatives, establish contacts, and zero in on special products or services. It's a concentrated approach."

Which way to go, shotgun or searchlight? If you're still in school, perhaps seeing as much as possible is the best approach. If you already know what you want, maybe you need to focus in on specific interests.

FINDING THE CONFERENCES

So, how do you find these conferences? Where do you look? Here are ten suggestions to get you started.

1. Look in the business section of your local newspaper.

2. Peruse trade and association journals.

3. Contact your local convention center.

4. Seek out local art supply outlets; they usually have passes.

5. Ask fellow students and your instructors.

6. Look for postings around campus.

7. Contact your local chamber of commerce.

8. Contact large hotels in your area with convention facilities.

9. Get on the Internet and look around.

10. Contact the National Trade Show Bureau at (303) 860-7626.

Try to attend at least one industry-related conference each year, even (particularly) while you're still in school. What you see, hear, touch, and get to know in half a day at such a show is an education all its own.

People
Who Are Doing It

MEET BARBARA LASZO

VITAL STATISTICS

Barbara, twenty-five, emigrated from her native Hungary in 1985. She attended Pasadena City College where she earned her associate degree in Art.

❑ PRESENT JOB

Interning 24 hours a week at Intervisual Books, Inc., in Santa Monica, California.

❑ POP-UP ART

"Intervisual Books is the largest pop-up book company in the world," says Barbara. "Here we take it from concept to finished product. And we do everything from *The Icky Sticky Frog* to *A History of the Harley Davidson Motorcycle Company*."

Barbara feels she is lucky to be interning at Intervisual Books because here, with 65 employees under one roof, she can get the whole picture—no pun intended. "Everyone is in the same building: writers, artists, designers, paper engineers, and packagers. It's a great opportunity for me to take it all in."

❏ FROM THE GET-GO—HER OWN PROJECT

The day Barbara arrived to begin her nonpaying internship she was given her very own project. "It was a bit intimidating," she says, "but I dug right in. I was essentially asked to design a children's book from scratch. I came up with the characters, did the storyboard, the layout, and the front cover. The illustrations themselves, however, were done by a freelance illustrator. Now I am on to a new project, another complete book."

❏ PORTFOLIO BUILDING

Barbara, as a result of her interning, has a better idea of what industry wants, and thus what she should be concentrating on in the future. "I now know how important computer skills are," she says. "I will need to beef up my coursework in that area when I get back to my classes. Also, here in particular, the ability to sketch quickly from my head is crucial. I have to work on that, too. Basically, as a result of my interning, I know better what to put in my portfolio."

While Barbara's interning experience at Intervisual Books is clearly a plus, she knows other students who have not been as fortunate. "It depends on what they make you do," she says. "If it's spending all your time at the copy machine, that's no good. Find out what you'll be doing ahead of time. That way you won't be disappointed."

MEET PAUL CUNINGHAM

VITAL STATISTICS

Paul is now a senior designer at Favermann Design, a firm specializing in environmental and graphics design. Six years ago, he began his internship at the studio. Though it has been a while since he interned, his experience was so rewarding that it remains vivid to this day.

❏ PRESENT JOB

Senior graphic designer at Favermann Design.

❏ OFFICE ETIQUETTE

"As an intern, what I learned more than anything was how to conduct myself in a professional environment," Paul says. "In school, you have deadlines, but in the real world, you may have seven to ten projects going at the same time. No one cares about the other one, just theirs. In school you can do everything from shouting across the room to running off to get a soda. Here it is more businesslike, more professional. There is office etiquette to follow."

❏ PORTFOLIO BUILDING

Paul also discovered that being an intern allowed him to develop a great professional portfolio. "You can tell the difference between a student's portfolio and a professional one from the first page," he says. "Often, a student portfolio will be too long. A lot of material is included that simply doesn't need to be there. A professional portfolio, one that includes work done on the job, is cleaner, neater, more focused."

❏ NOT ALL DESIGN FROM THE GET-GO

Not all the interns working at Favermann Design are major contributors, at least not at first. "We have a wide range," Paul explains. "There are some we give free rein to from the start. Others, we have emptying the trash and running for doughnuts. Even the latter, though, are learning. They are in the environment, overseeing what is happening. We let them sit in on meetings, watch presentations. If, as a firm, we have to constantly interact with an intern, we won't get anything done. What interns do here pretty much depends on what they are ready for. We take it from there."

A FEW KEY POINTS TO REMEMBER

- The internship experience lets you see all aspects of the work environment: the good, the bad, and the boring.
- An internship should be a fifty-fifty proposition; the student gets experience and the firm gets new ideas.
- Watch the interning no-no's while keeping a positive attitude.
- Co-op takes internship one step farther—to a paying job.
- The résumé's purpose is to get you a job interview, no more, no less.
- Your portfolio should represent samples of your work rather than long sections of many projects.
- Personal web sites that host on-line portfolios are becoming common.
- Animation, or work with similarly large data files, is often presented on a video reel.
- In the information interview, the purpose is to see and be seen.
- When attending industry conferences, go forth with a plan and a purpose.

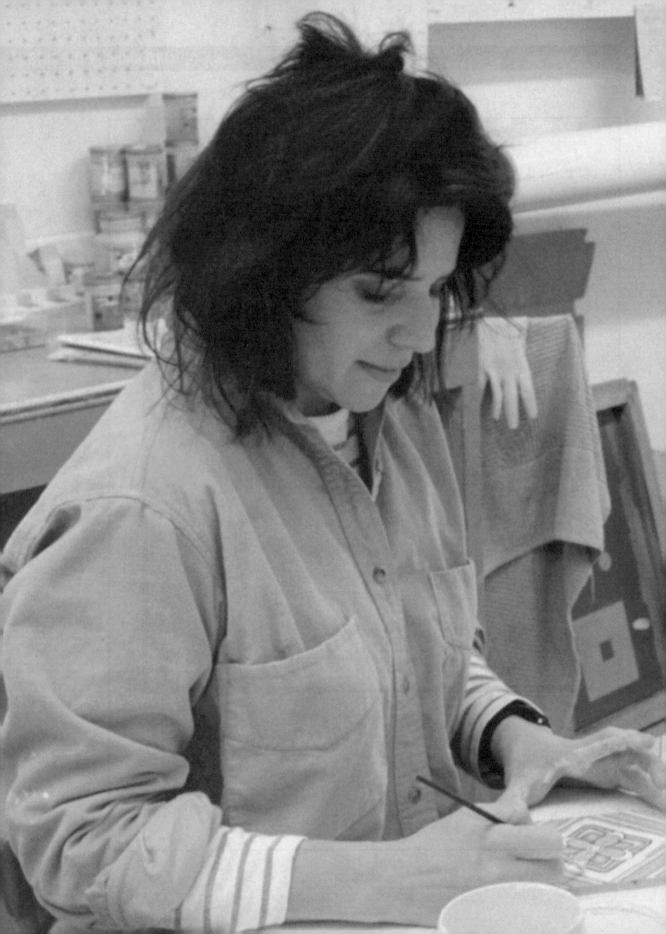

CHAPTER EIGHT

The Company Artist

"The difference between a design firm, an advertising agency, and an in-house department can be like night and day or day and day," says prolific author and re-aspected graphic designer Steve Heller. "Some offer very different services; others are very similar. Deciding which field is best is a personal choice."

Most artists and graphic designers, especially those in production, begin their careers working for someone else. They start out in house—that is, in graphic design departments at retail giants, manufacturing establishments, government agencies, and entertainment industries—anywhere art and graphic design is needed.

Others find immediate openings at design firms, from small, mom-and-pop enterprises to mega shops with more than 100 creatives. These companies are in the design business; that's what they do. If you wish to outsource your design needs, design firms are usually the folks to contact.

Actually, though, it depends on what you're looking for. For decades, graphic design has found a home, a reason to exist, in one industry above all others—advertising. So pervasive and encompassing is this industry's use of artists and graphic designers that it is fair to separate out advertising from design firms as a whole. Many art and graphic design students, upon graduation, seek immediate employment at advertising and marketing firms where they help to get a client's message out in traditional or new media.

In this chapter, we explore what it's like to work in house, at design firms and in ad agencies. We conclude by examining current compensation—who is making how much and where.

IN HOUSE

Working as an in-house artist or graphic designer, you are part of a corporate team. You may be a one-person show like Edwin Saravia, the graphic designer we met in Chapter Four, doing signage at a Home Depot outlet. Or you could be on the 17-person creative team at the Hasbro Corporate Creative Group, helping to develop materials for Poof and Puff Perfume. Either way, your purpose is to promote corporate products, services, and identity through art and graphic design.

BAD RAP

Working in house has its advantages. You are on salary, you usually work a 40-hour week, corporate career opportunities outside your specialty are available to you, and there are all those fringe benefits. You are, in short, a company person.

But being employed as a creative in a corporate environment has its downside, too. Some say working for one client only, promoting the same brand day in and day out, can be a real drag, particularly on your creativity. "I was always working on the same type of projects," says Jeff Stapleton, now senior art director at Graphica Design, a design firm in Dayton, Ohio. "If you work for Square-D, you could be doing their brochures forever. It can get stagnant."

"In-house people get burned out because they have one product they are designing for, or one group of products," says Theo Stephan Williams. "Consequently, the corporations do not attract the best designers. Those in house tend to be more marketing-focused people."

Add to this the supposed stifling effect of maintaining corporate standards, ever-present corporate politics, and the lack of respect that "goofy designers" are often subject to from others in the organization, and you see why working in house may not be for every creative.

Perhaps the real problem here is one of misconception? Maybe in-house design is getting a bum rap. While many refugees from the in-house wars are now happily working for design firms, ad agencies, or as freelancers, there are others who have found a creative and rewarding outlet right at home. Working in house need not be a downer.

STAYING CREATIVE

Anne Tryba loves parks, particularly theme parks, but that's not surprising. As head of the Graphic Design Department at Walt Disney Imagineering in Glendale, California, she is intimately involved with them. It is at Disney's Glendale facility that entire theme parks and resorts are planned, designed, and prototyped.

With 19 graphic designers on staff and more than twice that many on what is called staff extension, the Imagineering facility is an in-house design enterprise like no other. "There is a tremendous creative energy here all around," says Anne. "When surrounded with so many creative types, you are naturally inspired."

Still, even in this magic kingdom, Anne has to work to keep her designers on the leading edge. "We have projects that last a long, long time," she says. "How do you keep people motivated when they aren't likely to see results until opening day, down the road?"

One way Anne does just that is to hand out lots of miniprojects, to supplement long-term assignments. "It's sort of like freelancing for the designers," she declares. "It lets them branch out."

Sending her folks to conferences and seminars is another way Anne encourages her in-house people to stay fresh. "We also see to it that designers get out and about in the company, explore what else is going on, get a sense that they are a part of the big picture."

Clearly, working in house requires working—working at staying fresh, avoiding burnout. And while not every in-house creative is immersed in a design culture such as one finds at Disney, creativity exists regardless of the setting. Remember, a designer's approach and effort determine the reward and outcome. As one designer put it, "Being in house isn't the issue; inspiring and challenging oneself is."

DESIGN FIRMS

Working at a design firm, you are surrounded by art and graphic design and by those who generate it. Creatives are everywhere. Such firms seek clients—that is, other firms, companies, and institutions, public and private— and offer to satisfy some or all of their design needs on a contract basis. There is no excuse not to stay charged in a design studio environment.

Many design firms specialize; they provide expertise in a particular area of design. Favermann Design, for example, concentrates on environmental design—specializing in branding, way finding, and signage programs. Blumlein Associates, Inc. focuses on the design of exhibitions, environmental and print graphics, retail interiors, and graphical computer interfaces. Stuart Karten Design is a 15-year-old industrial design consultancy based in Los Angeles.

Other firms, however, offer a broad range of services, believing there is much overlap in all types of design. For artists and graphic designers working at such firms, this can be advantageous. They may be given wide exposure and an opportunity to develop expertise in many areas.

Design firms come in all sizes, too: small, medium, and large. Small is understood to include fewer than 5 individuals; medium, from 5 to 20; and large, anything over 20. Some nationally known design firms employ creative types by the hundreds, all across the country.

Let's examine what separates the different-sized design firms and, just as important, what they have in common.

TAKING CARE OF BUSINESS

John Sayles is owner of Sayles Graphic Design in Des Moines, Iowa. A graduate of Des Moines Technical High School and Des Moines Area Community College, he believes his training at both institutions prepared him well for success in a field he felt destined for from the age of six. "Growing up, art was what I excelled in," the now forty-two-year-old proprietor says. "It was art, design, photography, illustration, and printmaking six hours a day while in school."

Upon graduation, John worked at a number of ad agencies, eventually getting fired from most. "It wasn't what I wanted," he confesses. "They needed to make money—no problem there. But I thought I could make money and do good design, too. Fifteen years ago I put that belief to the test; I went out on my own."

As a small studio owner, John is as much a businessman as a designer, but he still gets down in the pits with everyone else. "I'm not into the big management thing like many colleagues my age who spend their time selling, bringing in the business," he says. "My love is art, using my hands."

But John knows how to think like a business owner. "You beat your competition before 8:00 A.M. and after 5:00 P.M.," he advises. "I see so many designers who aren't business oriented. They blow things off, forget to bill. With my art and the business end, I have the best of both worlds."

BEYOND THE BOUTIQUE

Steve Curry of Curry Design, Inc. finds his company in transition. "We are a medium-size shop—11 people—and growing fast," he says. "We'll be moving into a new, 6,000-square-foot warehouse in an upscale district. We have to. If you remain small, you'll crumble. Growth is the only way to survive."

Steve's firm is doing more corporate entertainment business these days, working with higher-budgeted clients. "We want to move from a boutique to more of an agency," he insists. "We could go broke doing the little projects."

In his rush to expand, Steve is prepared to hire anyone with talent. "Two-year graduates are fine," he says, "But they must not only have the skills, but also have a God-given gift. That, and a great attitude. We will take it from there—nurture them, teach them, take them under our wing."

Steve is particularly enthusiastic when lauding the advantages of working at a design firm rather than in house. "Here you build a broader portfolio," he says. "In house, you can get pigeonholed. If you have done only Disney home video packaging for your entire professional life, that can be a problem."

Steve also admits there are disadvantages to working at his place. "We have fewer benefits, no dental, and no discount tickets to parks. There *are* perks to the corporate life."

SOLVING PROBLEMS

At Graphica Design, variety is evident all around. From business to business, corporate identity, collateral literature, illustration, interactive media, CDs, and web sites, there isn't much they don't do. And their client list is as varied as their projects.

"On the conservative side," says Jeff Stapleton, senior art director of the 40-plus employee shop, "we work with such established, staid companies as Square-D and Crown Lift Trucks, but we also do design for Hasbro Toys and Disney stores. We are even developing back-to-school materials for the *Harry Potter* series.

While Graphica Design has not always sought out two-year program graduates when hiring, a degree is not as important as talent, Jeff is quick to acknowledge. "You can show me degrees all you want, but if it doesn't come true in your portfolio, then it's not there."

Talent itself is not enough, either. "The ability to get along, collaborate, is absolutely essential in a group our size," Jeff continues. "You can't always take all your goodies and go into a closet, shut the door, and then come out when you're finished. You have to be able to work in a group, take constructive criticism based on an art director's intuition, experience, or the desires of a client, regardless of how you feel. Ego suppression is a necessary (even if acquired) skill."

"Criticism is a gift if taken correctly," says Jack Anderson, founding partner of Hormall Anderson Design Works. "It's also a fact of life. If you push the limits, the boundaries, and continuously reinvent yourself you invite criticism. If you can't accept criticism, you've chosen the wrong business. Strive for a balance of ego and humility; confidence is the willingness to learn."

Miranda Moss, principal at Yamamoto/Moss, a design firm in Minneapolis, Minnesota with more than 100 creatives, agrees but adds, "When we hire, the candidate is questioned by three or four people, from the probable manager to the would-be teammate. I look for growth potential; does the candidate have enough interest in areas we are expanding into? I do personality assessments before hiring. These are the people we are going to rely on. But in the end, the thing I look for most is niceness. That's right—is this applicant a nice person?"

Compared to in-house design, working at a large design firm may be more intense. "We have hundreds of clients and they all must be served perfectly," adds Miranda. "In house, you may have many clients but it's one company. You have one big brand to keep. Our work is more client-dominated. We have our peaks and valleys, catering to a client's needs and demands. In house, the pace is more controlled."

Regardless of a design firm's size, when working with varied projects and clients, you are solving problems. Often you get to learn about industries across the board, from those that manufacture fuses to those creating the latest cartoon characters. Remember, helping to solve problems, designing a customer's packaging, their look—that's what it is all about. It is a problem-solving, creative field.

ADVERTISING AGENCIES

Advertising can be an expensive and risky form of communication. In a short period and using limited space, you must convey and communicate a positive message to sell a product or service.

Nonetheless, we are all aware how ever-present advertising is. And according to everyone who should know, it is predicted to be even more so in the future. As Jay Chiat, head of ScremingMedia, Inc., puts it: "TV and radio commercials, print ads, billboards, and taxi tops—none of it in the years to come will be plentiful enough to accommodate all the commercial messages that are agitating to get out. Advertising will of necessity slip beyond the boundaries of the 30-second commercial and the full-page ad and migrate to the rest of the world, including entertainment, journalism, and art. Eventually, every surface that can display a message will be appropriated for advertising."

A sobering and scary thought for some. Yet for others, those in the business of creating and conveying the selling message, there are opportunities galore.

BRAND BUILDERS

One such firm immersed in the advertising arena is Monsoon Microstudios, a high-billing Philadelphia outfit that has seen the benefit of exciting publicity of late. Featured in *How Magazine* and on CNN, the once-boutique shop has grown to acquire million-dollar accounts, allowing it to reach $60 million in billings in a recent year. "Initially, we were this cool, cutting-edge, youth-targeted ad agency," says Steve Puccia, chief development officer. "We still are. But we are glad to be taking on the more traditional brick-and-mortar firms—mortgage companies for example—as well."

Located in the city's low-income empowerment zone, Monsoon is not your typical Madison Avenue ad agency. "When we started, the average age around here was twenty-four or twenty-five," says Steve. "Now it has grown to thirty or thirty-one. I guess that's indicative of our moving to more staid clients."

That's not the only reason age is creeping up. In the beginning, Monsoon Microstudios just didn't have the money to recruit veterans. Now, as revenues have increased, they can look to people who can bring with them not only experience, but also a client base. As a result, Monsoon has gone from saying to their clients, "This is what we can do for you," to "This is what we have done for others."

With their slogan, "The Brand That Builds Brands," Monsoon positions itself as an agency that "feels your pain, knows where you're at." "If we can build our own brand from obscurity, we can do it for our clients, too," Steve announces.

THE SWASH SAYS IT ALL

A graduate of a two-year program at Queensborough Community College, in New York, Steve is a firm believer in what such programs can offer. "So many kids coming out of high school today just don't know where to go yet," he says. "Their friends head off to four-year schools and party, party, party—all the time incurring $10,000 loans."

So what does Monsoon look for in art and graphic design graduates? Evidently, a combination of advertising savvy, a unique perspective on the marketplace, and an understanding of brand building. You have to ask: What does it mean to take a company's logo and brand an image, promote the product? Clearly, there's a big difference between advertising a product and branding an image. As Steve concludes, "Nike is a good example. The swash says it all. That is company recognition—branding."

WHICH WAY TO GO?

So—in house, graphic design firm, or advertising agency? Of course, commitment to one does not preclude the others. Indeed, many creatives have worked in all three over a span of years.

What, in essence, are the advantages and disadvantages of each? Steve Heller has given the subject considerable thought, most notably in his book *Becoming a Graphic Designer*. In an e-mail to this writer, he shares his reflections:

> In house means you always work for someone else. But there are different kinds of in-house work and many job descriptions. . . . As a junior designer you are there to follow instructions of supervisors. This is a time to learn and acquire skills. The period of time spent as a junior might vary from one month to three years, depending on the firm and your value to the firm.
>
> The difference between a design firm, an advertising agency, and an in-house department can be like night and day or day and day. Some offer very different services, others are very similar. Deciding which field is best is a personal choice. Advertising as a rule is very service-oriented and dictated by often irrational marketing concerns. Graphic design

firms are not as limited or proscribed, but it all depends on the quality of the clients and how the principals choose to practice design. A good designer will provide hours of invaluable education. A bad one, well . . . you get the picture.

BRINGING HOME THE DOUGH

Every other year *How Magazine* conducts an extensive business salary survey, looking into the monetary state of affairs in the art and graphic design professions. Their Y2K survey shows mixed results.

Overall, average salaries for the graphic design profession are up nearly 6 percent compared to two years previous, but bonuses are down significantly.

Generally, the survey tells us that men still make more than women, by $10,000 a year. Designers in cities like San Francisco and New York earn more than those in St. Louis or Dallas. And in-house designers average $12,000 less per year than their design-firm counterparts, though the former are saddled with fewer management responsibilities. Finally, age and experience still count, winning out over youth and inexperience.

Specifically, the annual salary for those working in an in-house corporate design department was $44,252. Those at an ad agency earned $51,005. And at design firms, the compensation was highest: $56,414.

Geography does, indeed, matter. If you live in the north central region of the country, expect an average income of $45,221. In the South you'll earn $47,993. Out west, you will pull down $50,606. And in the Northeast, which includes New York City, of course, you will be paid the most: $53,308. Keep in mind, however, that along with higher salaries you can expect a higher cost of living.

Principals/partners/owners took home an average of $66,074, according to survey results. Art directors/creative directors pulled in $53,127. Senior designers/web designers/designers earned an average of $40,753, while entry-level designers/production artists/web programmers saw an average compensation of $30,775.

Finally, as mentioned above, experience does count. Those with less than five years in the profession earned an average of $38,149. Those on the job from six to ten years were pulling in an average of $48,138. If you were a seasoned pro with 11 to 15 years experience, you earned $52,388 on average. And those with more than 15 years at work received salaries of $70,175.

For a complete report on *How*'s salary results, visit their web site at *www.howdesign.com.*

Understand, within specific subfields of art and graphic design, compensation varies considerably. For example, though in an established industry, where entry is difficult, animation and digital effects can be quite rewarding, monetarily. According to a 1997–1998 SkillsNet survey, clean-up artists averaged $54,600; character animators, $106,900; and art directors, a whopping $153,400 a year. Yes, there is money to be made in art and graphic design.

However, if that's what it's all about for you, you may be in the wrong profession. Sure, you should be compensated as well as possible for your talent, education, training, and skill. Unfortunately, in a competitive field where supply always seems to exceed demand, that is not necessarily the case. Of course, you could go into business for yourself as a freelancer. Theoretically, your income will know no bounds. In Chapter Nine, we see if that is, indeed, the case.

COMPANIES THAT ARE DOING IT

Here are a few in-house design groups, graphic design studios, and advertising agencies to note.

[Metal] Studio
http://wwwmetalstudio.com
Starting out with just one woman working out of her apartment, this studio in Houston, Texas now has 12 employees, including graphic designers, web developers, and two staffers whose sole job is to "bring in the business."

Hasbro Corporate Creative Group
http://www.hasbro.com
Made up of a 17-member in-house creative team located in a 300,000-square-foot, refurbished mill, Hasbro Toys isn't playing around with its art and graphic design department.

Steve Morris Design
http://www.stevenmorrisdesign.com
Built on the mantra "Serious Fun," Steve and his firm are constantly promoting the studio and going after larger clients, one of which is Hasbro Toys.

FrogDesign
http://www.frogdesign.com
One of the largest and most respected design firms, Frog is a multidisciplinary shop covering graphic and industrial design, new-media know-how, and branding.

Via
http://www.vianow.com
A large, multifaceted, five-office, eighty-employee operation, Via specializes in good business design.

J.J. Sedelmaier Productions, Inc.
A firm specializing in advertising, Sedelmaier does design for Hallmark Cards, among many other clients.

Paraham Santana, Inc.
This ad agency did an ad for Spike Lee that earned an award from *How Magazine*.

People
Who Are Doing It

MEET SCOTT WREN

VITAL STATISTICS

Scott Wren, thirty-three, is living the graphic artist's dream, working for Disney's Imagineering in Southern California. Raised in Houston, Texas, he got his start as a medical illustrator at the Baylor College of Medicine. Today, theme parks are his passion, having worked on Animal Kingdom in Florida and Disney's California Adventure in Anaheim. Given the company's commitment to building more theme parks, Scott's continued employment prospects look good indeed.

❏ PRESENT JOB

Graphic designer, Disney's Imagineering.

❏ ALL IN THE FAMILY

"With both parents graphic designers, I wasn't about to become a plumber," says Scott. Following in their footsteps, he began work as a medical illustrator right out of high school. "What started out as a summer job turned into a five-year gig," Scott says, "but then I realized I needed formal training. I took off for art school in Florida. I then entered an apprenticeship program with Disney. I've never looked back."

❏ GOING 3-D

What Scott likes most about working at Disney is seeing his art turn into three-dimensional objects. But he didn't leap into creating the cool stuff right out of college. No, Scott had to serve his apprenticeship first. "Two months after arriving in California, they shipped me back to Florida," he says. "I spent nine months there, on site, out in the field, installing all the signage for Animal Kingdom. My background was in print. This was all new to me. I was definitely in the mentoring mode."

When asked to explain what is exciting about his work, Scott responds simply, "It's Disney." But he isn't mesmerized by the name, recognizing that working at the Imagineering facility is not all fun, fun, fun. "At one point, you understand it's a job like any other," he insists. "You get up every morning, drive to work, put in eight or nine hours, and go home." Yes, even in the Magic Kingdom, it's all in a day's work.

MEET KATHERINE JOHNS

VITAL STATISTICS

Katherine Johns has experienced practically all aspects of her firm's business. She started on the print side, taking the prepress catalogs on through the printing and binding process. Katherine then moved to Los Angeles, where she worked in advertising management for five years. Back to shopnow.com, Katherine now manages their on-line department.

❏ PRESENT JOB

On-line department manager for *shopnow.com*.

❏ GROWING CLIENT LIST

Shopnow.com creates catalogs for its clients. "We do everything from concept through design to copyediting," says Katherine. "We do all the photography in house, all of the production using QuarkXPress, and the entire printing."

The firm has an impressive client list: Starbucks, L.L. Bean, Discovery Channel, Hallmark Cards, Hickory Farms—names we all recognize.

To accomplish what they do, concept to production of catalogs, *shopnow.com* employs seventy people. They have six art directors, three creative directors, two creative managers, and a host of support and production people. When hiring production people, they look mainly for experience. As Katherine says, "At this company, it is all about knowing QuarkXPress. If they know that, we'll bring them on."

❏ THE FREELANCING LIFE—NOT

"I can sell my company's products, but not myself," Katherine volunteers. "I just don't have the personality for it. Besides, I need to know where my next check is coming from. I don't want to always be looking for the next gig. I could never freelance."

There are advantages to working at a corporate agency that you might not have considered, Katherine is quick to point out. "With freelancers, contractors, you see them for a few days maybe, and that's it. They're not doing lunch with us; there is no opportunity to develop friendships. Here at the firm, we go out for drinks, party at each other's houses. It is a different atmosphere. I guess I am a company person."

MEET THOMAS ROSSMAN

VITAL STATISTICS

Tom Rossman is one of three principals in the advertising agency of RLR Advertising & Marketing. While in college, he studied exhibit, furniture, graphic, and product design.

❏ PRESENT JOB

Principal in RLR Advertising & Marketing, a medium-size advertising agency with $15 million in annual billings.

❏ GIVING IT AWAY

In advertising, design is often free—that is, design is provided as a service free of charge, as long as the client buys into other services the firm can provide. "There is nothing new in this," says Tom. "Take exhibition design, for example. Many trade show display companies will throw in the design free in order to get a contract to actually build the booth."

You have a similar situation in advertising. "The real money is made on your commission in buying the media: print, TV, radio," Tom explains. "In graphic design, on the other hand, all you are selling is your time. In advertising, you can do one ad and make a lot of money, especially if it's placed in every magazine in America. With graphic design, you get paid the same amount whether the client prints one thousand or one million brochures."

❏ DOING IT THEMSELVES

As with engineering, today's art directors and senior graphic designers often find themselves (thanks to the computer) doing work themselves, turning out production material. In engineering, the draftsperson as a separate job category has all but vanished. Working drawings are turned out by the engineer. While there is plenty for production artists and graphic designers to do (few supervisors are going to take the time to learn Maya or Flash), some find it easier to do the less-involved work themselves. "Design departments used to be structured into creative sections and production sections," says Tom. "A designer would do the sketch and pass it over to the layout person. There's no need for that anymore. What to do? Production people must learn design."

❑ PROBLEM SOLVERS

"Because of the computer, we turn out far more work with fewer people than ever before," says Tom. "We also interact less with the client directly. Now we just send over the PDF files."

So what are advertising firms looking for when hiring artists and graphic designers? "Problem solvers," Tom declares. "Folks enroll in these certificate programs, yet all they really teach them is the computer. They don't teach them how to become designers. Design has always been about problem solving."

A FEW KEY POINTS TO REMEMBER

• Working in house has its advantages: You are on salary, you usually work a 40-hour week, and other corporate career opportunities are open to you.
• Staying creative in an in-house environment, where you may do much the same thing day in and day out, is a challenge.
• If you are working at a design studio, it helps to have a business sense.
• Ego suppression is something every designer must strive to achieve.
• At an ad agency, you work to build a client's brand.
• Advertising is service-oriented, often dictated by irrational marketing concerns.
• Overall, average salaries for graphic designers are up.

CHAPTER NINE

Freelancing

Once you get locked into a firm and are forced to produce work for a paying client, creativity is not necessarily a priority. The accounting and business side takes over. As a freelancer, you are often brought in to provide something new, something fresh. You are hired for your creativity.

Ah, the freelancing life. Brought on board by other artists, in-house organizations, design firms, and advertising agencies to solve their most vexing problems, as a freelancer you are your own boss, free to choose the work you want to do when you want to do it, for pay befitting your status as a businessperson, an entrepreneur. In business for yourself, and respected for your unique artistic and design talents, you are living the American dream; you are in control.

After all, who wouldn't want to get up late in the morning—or not at all? Take a vacation anytime? Go shopping in midday instead of after work with everyone else? Never get fired? Live anywhere in the country—at the beach or in a mountain cabin? And have virtually no commute? The list goes on, but you get the picture. The bottom line? You're the boss, you do whatever you want, whenever you want.

So is the image, the fantasy. Reality, as we shall see shortly, is another matter.

From the two words, "free" and "lance," the original freelancers were just that: knights of old who sold their services to a nobleman, party, state, or cause. With the job done, they were available for the next battle or gig, to whomever offered the best deal.

Today's freelance artists and graphic designers operate in much the same way, with the lance replaced by a pencil, brush, or computer. Companies reluctant to hire permanent staff artists or designers often turn to freelancers to fill their immediate needs.

Some argue, however, that given the commercial nature of art and graphic design in the twenty-first century, freelancing is less a choice than a work style thrust upon creatives, like it or not. Given the project nature of the multimedia industry in particular, jobs are usually temporary. Many companies hire independent contractors, freelancers, to supplement their work force.

That's great, you say. Work aplenty for freelancers! Yes—perhaps. On the downside, however, there may be no alternative. Thus, whether you plan to make freelancing your full-time gig or not, as an artist or graphic designer you're likely to freelance for at least some time in the years to come. Knowing the pros and cons of the freelance life is, therefore, important for everyone working in art and graphic design.

TO THE RESCUE

Elena Welsh started her freelance career six years ago, doing work in publishing, mainly for Henry Holt & Company. Today, it's advertising brochures, books, and plenty of web work: banner ads, jump pages, and e-mail advertising. "Now I work more directly with the client rather than through an ad agency," Elena says. "I started out with the agencies, going on site for them, and eventually I set up my own home office. I now do most of my work only a few feet from where I sleep."

Elena loves putting out the fires—saving the day, so to speak. "The client is behind on a deadline; you are called in to turn things around. Often you are the hero, the expert that makes it all okay. It's a great feeling. But to make that happen, you'd better be prepared to burn the midnight oil. It can be 18-hour days for a week or two, followed by total downtime."

Tom Banaro is basically a self-taught artist. "I took a few courses at De Anza Community College, back in the mid-seventies," he says. "But for the most part, it has been an intuitive thing. I started applying my aesthetics, shopping my art around, and doing free work for publications just to get work exposed."

No longer working for free, Tom is now called in to bring something to the table. "They are looking for a different point of view, something that isn't going on in house," he says. "Artists can create a niche for themselves by developing a personal style."

"If you don't mind riding a roller coaster, freelancing can be great," adds Geoffery Smith, a freelancer in Dayton, Ohio. "While it can be frustrating, I personally love it. I enjoy working on the edge, wondering what is going to happen next. True, it is nice when a job comes in that will eat up a couple of months of my time, but more typically, I simply can't forecast anything more than two weeks in advance. That's about as far out as I can see."

Not all organizations, of course, can use the services of a freelancer. In many advertising firms, it is hard to employ them. Things move so fast, by the time a firm calls in a freelancer, the project is due. If such agencies had bigger projects, more long-term, it might be different.

AS GOOD AS YOUR LAST JOB

Working freelance, you are working for yourself—and for someone else. There is, after all, always a client. What do they want from you? What, for them, makes a great freelancer?

"It differs so much in our industry," says Theo Stephan Williams, "because the business is so diverse. The key is to be able to pick up quickly on the client's needs. Not being on staff, that can be difficult. The more successful freelancers, however, are good at it."

Christian Ikeda, of Diana Slavin Women's Wear, has found such a free-lancer in Tom Banaro. She can't stop singing his praises. "We put a lot of trust in Tom because he knows us, our style, our needs, so well," she says. "He has worked with us for so long we don't have to start from ground zero every time. The quality of his work is great, and he is so reliable. We know he will come through."

Katherine Johns, of *shopnow.com*, is in a similar situation with Elena. "We can always count on her," Katherine says, "but that's not the case with all free-lancers I have known. Let's face it—it's not as though they are going to lose their job. If a design presentation is due on Monday but they don't feel like working on the weekend, they just don't. Not with Elena; she always goes the extra mile. Elena once said, 'I felt it was important to the presentation to have copy here, so I wrote this myself.' I love things like that." Who wouldn't!

Bottom line? Freelancing is the ability to come through. Remember, professionalism is everything. You're only as good as your last job.

HUSTLE, HUSTLE, HUSTLE

Being good—that is, being a terrific artist or designer who also has great people skills—is only part of what it takes to succeed as a freelancer. You must also be a smart businessperson. "That has not always been the case in our profession," says Dave Lesh, a 20-year veteran freelancer living in Indianapolis. "We simply aren't the best businesspeople in the world and it's hurting us."

You don't have to have the business skills of a Bill Gates to take care of business, but taking care of business is a must. "I tell freelancers that before you even go into a project, make sure you get the 'no-fun' stuff out of the way," advises Theo. "Meet with the accountant, determine how you are going to bill, negotiate everything up front. For most creatives, the business end is a downer, but it's work that has to be done."

"Fortunately for me," says Geoffery, "I was raised by an accountant. I have always known how to keep the books. I make it simple, pay my taxes on time, and follow up on bills not paid. You have to."

"It is a hassle, no question about it," says Tom Banaro. "Not just in the running of the business, but in getting business. Until you can sit back and wait for the work to come to you, you will be out hustling most of the time."

WITH A LITTLE HELP FROM MY REP

If you don't want (or don't have the time) to go out and bring it in, there is an alternative. Many independent artists and graphic designers employ what are known as artists' representatives to represent their interests to the outside world. The reps' job is to get work for creatives, and in the best of circumstances, help them build a career. Of course, for such services they are paid a fee, usually in the form of a 20 to 30 percent commission on each job contracted for.

Scott Hull, of Scott Hull Associates, is such a representative, one who considers himself a manager of artists more than a mere broker for their services. "We represent Mary Grandpré, the illustrator for all the *Harry Potter* books," he says. "Instead of grabbing onto her short-term success and exploiting it for immediate advantage, we are planning long term. We want to turn her artwork into a product, her philosophy into a brand. Scott Hull Associates is in it with her for the long haul."

Geoffery, who has been working with Scott for more than seven years now, is also in it for the stretch. He feels he could get by without a rep, but why should he? If a rep brings in business and negotiates contracts above what you would earn on your own, then his worth is obvious. At least that's how Geoffery sees it.

Getting a rep to take you on is a challenge in itself, however. As in publishing, where finding a literary agent is as difficult as finding a publisher, so it is for grabbing an artist's representative. "First, I look for talent," Scott says. "And I want to know how deep it goes; I want to see an art style that is timeless. Second, there is attitude. I need to sense a bit of an ego, but not too much. The artist has to have drive, passion. Today, even though the industry is full of artists and product, I am concentrating on the talent I represent. I can't take on anyone new right now."

That's okay with Elena; she's so busy and well connected that she simply doesn't need the services of a rep. "For me, word of mouth is working," she says. "Because I spent so much time at various agencies, getting to know photographers, copywriters, other designers, I now get a lot of referrals. I will do a convention booth for a company and another firm will want to know who designed it. My work is getting out by itself."

In the end, reps like Scott simply use their extensive network of contacts to match the talent they represent with jobs to be done. Many freelance artists and graphic designers would simply not find enough work to sustain themselves without such reps.

A COMPETITIVE ENVIRONMENT

While Theo, Elena, and Geoffery have made freelancing a success, though none of them got there overnight and all must forever stay on top of their game, there are other artists and graphic designers—good ones—for whom the freelance life is not to be.

"I am trying to get out of the business," says Josef Gast, a graphic designer in Seattle, Washington. "As far as illustration is concerned, I think the business is dead. Stock illustration is one reason, but that's not all. With art directors adept at Photoshop and Illustrator, they are doing a lot of work themselves. I am trying to pick up an art director's job—what I used to do. I can't imagine anyone actually trying to make a living as a freelancer."

Josef is particularly critical with regard to agents. "My agent has a lot of people who are really young, just starting out," he says. "The agent tells them, 'Just hang in there for a few more years; you will make it.' So you're hot for a few years. After that, it cools down."

What is the reason for this state of affairs? Why are some freelance artists and designers turning away business while others are so hungry?

"Anyone with $3,000 can buy a page in a sourcebook and call themselves an illustrator," laments Dave Lesh, an active freelancer. "Right now, the market is flooded with imagery as well as people willing to produce it. And look at all the schools that have opened up in just the last 20 years. Everyone wants to be a graphic designer."

Yes, competition is keen. As we said at the beginning of this book and have repeated throughout, if you want a career as a commercial artist or graphic designer, you will be entering a field where supply has always exceeded demand. Yet, that demand is taking us in directions (the Web, for example) unimagined even five years ago. For those grounded in the basics, expert in the use of the new technology, and who have an entrepreneurial spirit, drive, and ability, there is definitely work to be done. Freelancing is not for the semiretired, part-time, catch-as-catch-can crowd. Freelancing requires a complete commitment in an artistic and business sense. With that dedication, much is possible.

GOING FOR IT

So, when to start, when to begin as a freelancer? There is much to be said for waiting, getting experience in an in-house firm, at a design studio, at an ad agency. "You need at least three years of work after college before you can even consider freelancing," insists Scott. "It requires maturity, a business savvy."

Theo isn't so sure one must wait. "I encourage artists to start freelancing as soon as they feel they can," she says. "The principal of our firm started freelancing right out of college. True, he was raised in an entrepreneurial family. I was twenty-three when I began freelancing. It is about ability. It really doesn't matter how young you are."

Perhaps not. Yet Austin, heading for his local community college in the fall, isn't thinking like a freelancer quite yet. He just wants to get started with the fundamentals of design and an introduction to Flash. And that, perhaps, is as it should be. But as Austin goes forth to pursue a career in art and graphic design, he would be wise to remember what a renowned Brooklyn, New York, Lincoln High School graphics instructor, Leon Friend, said about the profession long ago. According to Steve Heller, in his book *Design Literacy Continued*, Leon cautioned his students as follows:

> The essential factors in successful graphic expression are a knowledge of tradition of the craft (though not a slavish nor an academic one), a consideration of the purpose for which the design is intended, imagination, and a control of the requisite skill that will leave the artists free for self expression.

Valuable thoughts, not only for all the Austins starting out, but for those who are well on their way. After all, choosing a career in art and graphic design will require you to constantly reinvent yourself—just like the profession.

COMPANIES THAT ARE DOING IT

Here are a few artists and graphic designers making it as freelancers, though none of them ever got a free ride. All have struggled to get where they are now. All have to keep working to stay there.

John Ceballos   1047 Broadmoor Drive, Napa, CA 94558; (707) 226-1026
Former art director for Hallmark Greeting Cards; freelance illustrator for nine years specializing in editorial/humorist-type work.

David Lesh   (213) 548-3178
Founder of *illustatorspartnership.com*, an organization to promote the interests of independent illustrators.

Geoffrey Smith   217 Greendale Drive, Dayton, OH 45429; (937) 294-2288
Freelance illustrator with a simple, direct business approach.

Linda Souders   555 Buena Vista West, #702, San Francisco, CA 94117; (415) 252-5820
Freelance designer/art director specializing in direct-mail projects. She has been freelancing for ten years.

Theo Stephan Williams   (805) 344-4525
Founded Real Art Design Group, Inc. in 1985. Author of numerous books on freelancing.

People
Who Are Doing It

MEET JOHN CEBALLOS

VITAL STATISTICS

Right out of school, John went to work for Hallmark Greeting Cards. "It was somewhat stifling," he recalls, "but they provided a comfort zone. However, after five years, I realized I could spend my entire existence on earth working in this environment. I looked at my colleagues and began to see wrinkles forming. I needed to get out on my own, do the freelance thing."

❑ PRESENT JOB

Freelance artist and graphic designer.

❑ ME AND MY REP

For John, an artist's representative is extremely important. "Time and time again I will be called in by a client, then asked to come up with a monetary figure for my services," he says. "Yet, living in my own vacuum, I'm not sure what to charge. After I talk over the job, I give the information to my rep. He usually comes up with legitimate reasons why the figure should be double, maybe even ten times, what I was thinking."

A good rep, John believes, looks at pricing from the usage point of view. How much will the client benefit from his work? The freelancer, on the other hand, concentrates on how long it took him or her to produce the artwork or design. "That's wrong," John says. "That's why I have a rep. He gives me a different perspective."

❏ NO VACATION

While John admits it's nice to work anytime, day or night, in reality that may mean day *and* night. "Though it infuriates my wife, I have to take the phone with me everywhere, even on vacation," he says. "I cannot risk being out of touch for a week and as a result lose a good assignment. I need the option of accepting or turning down an assignment. The job is always there; it has to be."

Does John fear the unknown, the lack of a steady income? You bet. "I deal with that fear," he says, "by accepting too much work. But I shouldn't be whining, the checks are coming in. Better too much than too little."

❏ DIVERSITY IS KEY

His willingness to engage in varied projects is one reason John is so successful as a freelancer. On a given day, for example, he did the final sketches for a medical magazine, designed a clothing name tag, produced a product illustration for an on-line restaurant, and created a design for Johnson & Johnson. "No day is the same," John says. "Solving problems, it is what I love to do."

MEET LINDA SOUDER

VITAL STATISTICS

Linda would have started her freelancing career earlier, but an earthquake got in the way. "I moved to San Francisco the day of the 1989 earthquake," she says. "As the city recovered from that catastrophe, the recession hit. As a result of both, it was hard for me to get into freelancing. I wound up taking a staff job for three years first. But that gave me a ton of contacts, ones I used when I finally did take the plunge."

❏ PRESENT JOB

Freelance designer, working primarily in print.

❏ FLEXIBILITY IS WHAT IT'S ALL ABOUT

Linda has never liked being at a certain place at a certain time every day. As a freelancer, she has plenty of freedom to work as she wants, providing that she works, of course. "I feel that if working as a freelancer is good for me, it is also good for the client," Linda says. "If I am in a good mode, feeling free, my creativity goes up. The client benefits from that."

But there is a downside, she is quick to admit. "If you are on staff, you concentrate on the design; that's it. As a freelancer, you must juggle many balls. Your focus is often on other things, like running the business." Nonetheless, for Linda the compromise is just fine. "The freedom is well worth the added frustration of dealing with the marketing, the business end of things."

❏ DEALING WITH TOUGH TIMES

Linda believes these are good times to be a graphic designer, but she has experienced the bad periods, too. "When things are off, and the business isn't coming in as I would like it to, I ask myself two questions," she says. "What factors are beyond my grasp? Which ones are within my reach that I must fine-tune? If you are going into freelancing, it must be for the long haul. You need to find a way to ride out the ups and downs, and concentrate on what you can control. Staying on top of your art, always improving your skills— that's the answer."

A FEW KEY POINTS TO REMEMBER

- For some in art and graphic design, freelancing is not an option; it is the only choice.
- As a freelancer, you are often called in to turn things around.
- Working freelance, you work for yourself—and for someone else.
- In freelancing, professionalism is everything.
- Freelancers must also take care of business—their own.
- An artist's representative should help you build your career as a freelancer.
- Getting a rep to take you on is a challenge in itself.
- Freelancing is not for everyone, especially those just starting out in art and graphic design.
- This may be the best time in a long time to be a freelance artist or graphic designer.

Resources

PUBLICATIONS

Books, magazines, and journals in the fields of art and graphic design tend to be pricey. That's understandable; most are printed in full color, on quality stock. Still, it is important to begin building a library as soon as possible.

One way to avoid high book prices is to subscribe to a book club. Such clubs offer considerable discounts on a wide selection of items. If you follow the club's instructions carefully, and have the discipline to return monthly selection requests in a timely manner, a subscription may be to your advantage. Below is a list of two such book clubs. Also included is a list of the more popular and relevant magazines and journals you will want to at least look at, if not subscribe to.

BOOK CLUBS

Computer Graphics & Animation Book Club
P.O. Box 6304
Indianapolis, IN 46209-8310
Web site: *cga.booksonline.com*

Graphic Design Book Club
P.O. Box 12526
Cincinnati, OH 45212-0526
(800) 937-0963.

MAGAZINES AND JOURNALS

AIGA Journal of Graphic Design
(212) 807-1990
Web site: *www.aiga.org*

Design Graphics
(800) 688-6247
Web site: *subs@designgraphics.com.au*

EFX Art & Design
+31-522-261-303
Web site: *http://www.efxmag.com*

How Magazine
(513) 283-0963
Web site: *www.howdesign.com*

I.D. The International Design Magazine
(212) 447-1400
Web site: *www.IDonline.com*

Impress
(800) 2-KINKOS
Web site: *www.kinkos.com*

IS, Interiors & Sources
(312) 867-0019
Web site: *www.ISdesignNet.com*

Print
(212) 463-0600
Web site: *http://www.printmag.com*

Step by Step Graphics
(309) 688-2300

Wallpaper
(212) 533-9672
Web site: *www.wallpaper.com*

PROFESSIONAL ORGANIZATIONS

Many professional organizations exist for the benefit of commercial artists and graphic designers. A number have special memberships for students. Joining such organizations can help you in a number of ways:

- Through their continuing education programs, you can further your education.

- Invaluable networking opportunities open up.

- Professional organizations are a place to meet like-minded individuals who are experiencing the struggles and triumphs of the profession, just as you are.

Here is a list of professional organizations you might want to look into.

AIGA, American Institute of Graphic Arts
1059 Third Avenue
New York, NY 10021
(212) 752-0813

ASID, American Society of Interior Designers
608 Massachusetts Avenue NE
Washington, DC 20002
(202) 546-3480
Web site: *www.asid.usa.org*

Association of Graphic Communications
330 Seventh Avenue, 9th Floor
New York, NY 10001-5010
(212) 279-2100
Web site: *www.agcomm.org*

Association of Professional Model Makers
6502 Shiner Street
Austin, TX 78729
(512) 257-0730
Web site: *www.modelmakers.org*

Broadcast Designers Association
130 West 67th Street, Suite 25C
New York, NY 10023-5914
(212) 873-5014

FIDER, Foundation of Interior Design Education Research
60 Monroe Center, NW, #300
Grand Rapids, MI 49503
(616) 458-0400
Web site: *www.fider.org*

Graphic Arts Guild
90 John Street, #403
New York, NY 10083
(212) 791-3400
Web site: *www.gag.org*

**IDSA, Industrial Designers Society
of America**
1142 Walder Road
Great Falls, VA 22066
(703) 759-0100
Web site: *www.idsa.org*

**IOPP, Institute of Packaging
Professionals**
481 Carlisle Drive
Herndon, VA 20170
(703) 318-8970
Web site: *www.packinfo-world.org*

**National Computer Graphics
Association**
2722 Merrilee Drive, #200
Fairfax, VA 22031
(703) 698-9600

**SIGGRAPH, Special Interest Group
on Computer Graphics**
L.A. ACM/SIGGRAPH
P.O. Box 9399
Marina del Rey, CA 90295
(312) 321-6830
Web site: *www.siggraph.org*

**SPAR, Society of Photographers and
Artists Representatives**
60 East 42nd Street, Suite 1166
New York, NY 10165
(212) 779-7464

Index

A

A Brothers & Associates, 103
Active, 83
AD Cook and Associates, 26
Admedia, 11
Advanced Media Design,
   103
Advertising, 44
  agencies, 135–137,
    144–145
Alien Grafix, 62
Always Open, 62
Amplifier Creative, 11
Animation, 7, 17–18,
   53–55, 63–64
Animator, 9
Architectural Collaborative,
   103
Art:
  directors, 53
  range, 3
ArtDept USA, The, 103
Artists, 51–69
  animation, 7, 9, 53–55
  art directors, 53
  art-techno world, 6–7
    opportunities, 8–10
  book illustration, 59–61
  calligraphy, 12–13
  CD-ROM game design, 7
  commercial:
    artists, 1–16
    photographers, 10, 72,
      75–77
  companies, 129–145
    advertising agencies,
      135–137, 144–145
    brands, 136
    creativity, maintaining,
      131–132
    design firms, 132–135

graphic designer,
   141–142
  salaries, 138–139
comprehensive art, 56–57
computer game design, 7,
   9
digital photography, 7
display, 92
electronic illustration, 7
fashion illustration,
   55–57, 64–65
game:
  design, 53–55
  tester, 55
graphic:
  artist, 1–16, 52
  designer, 52
illustration, 67–69
interior designer, 10
Internet communications,
   7
jewelry design, 14–15
on-line magazines, 8
photographer, 13–14
script writers, 53
signage, 57–58, 66–67
starving, beyond the
   myth, 1–16
storyboard artists, 53
web site (page) designer,
   8–10, 72–75
Art-techno world, 6–7
  opportunities, 8–10
Artworks Graphic Design,
   26
AV Design/Media Maker, 11

B

Bachelor's degree, 35
Baggs Studio, 11
Bent Media, 83
Book:
  clubs, 161
  illustration, 59–61
Brackett-Zimmermann
    Associates, 26
Brands, 136
Butera School of Art, 42–43

BW Design, 83

C

Cabrillo Community College
   Desktop Publishing
   and Multimedia
   Program, 47
Calligraphy, 12–13
CD-ROM game design, 7
Ceballos, John, 154–156
Center for Digital Imaging
   and Sound, 47
Chester Lake Creations, 62
CLIK Productions, 26
Colorado Institute of Art,
   48
Colorgraphic Signs, 11
Commercial:
  art versus fine art, 3–4
  artists, 1–16
  photographer, 10, 72,
    75–77
Company artist, 129–145
  advertising agencies,
    135–137, 144–145
  brands, 136
  creativity, maintaining,
    131–132
  design firms, 132–135
  graphic designer,
    141–142
  salaries, 138–139
Comprehensive art, 56–57
Computer:
  design tool, 17–31
    electronic paintbrush,
      24–25
    HTML, 21
    kinematics, 19
    sculpting, 20
    techno animations,
      22–24
    WYSIWYG, 20–21
  game design, 7, 9
Conferences, 121–123
Connecticut Institute of
   Art, 43–44
Cooperative education, 116

Creative Media Development, 27
Creativity, 44–45
  maintaining, 131–132
Croquis, 65
Custom 3-D Graphics, 27

D

Design:
  CD-ROM game, 7
  computer game, 7, 9
  exhibit, 92, 97–100, 106–107
  firms, 132–135
  game, 7, 9, 53–55
  graphic, 52, 71–89, 141–142
  interior, 10, 92, 100–102, 107–108
  jewelry, 14–15, 92–94, 104–105
  package, 72, 78–80, 86–87
  product, 91–109
  tool, computer, 17–31
  toy, 92, 94–97, 105–106
  web page, 8–10, 72–75, 84–85
Digital photography, 7, 75–77
Display artist, 92
DPD Institute, 33–34

E

Education, 33–49
  advertising, 44
  art institutes, 47
  bachelor's degree, 35
  cooperative, 116
  creativity, 44–45
  industry requirements, 36–38
  regional occupational programs, 34
  sign painting, 42–43

See also: specific schools and programs
Electronic:
  illustration, 7
  paintbrush, 24–25
Elemental form, 14–15
Exhibit designer, 92, 97–100, 106–107

F

Fashion illustration, 55–57, 64–65
Fine art versus commercial art, 3–4
Food photographer, 85–86
Form, elemental, 14–15
FreeForm, 20
Freelancing, 147–159
  competition, 152–153
  using a representative, 151–152
FrogDesign, 140
Function, 51

G

Game:
  design, 53–55
  CD-ROM, 7
  computer, 7, 9
  tester, 55
Graphic:
  artist, 1–16, 52
  designer, 52, 71–89, 141–142
    commercial photographers, 72, 75–77
    digital photography, 75–77
    food photographer, 85–86
    multimedia, 72, 80–82, 88
    package design, 72, 78–80, 86–87
    stock photography, 86

web page design, 72–75, 84–85

H

Hasbro Corporate Creative Group, 140
HTML (Hypertext Markup Language), 21

I

Illustration, 67–69
  electronic, 7
Illustrators, 51–69
  animation, 53–55
  art directors, 53
  book, 59–61
  comprehensive art, 56–57
  fashion, 55–57, 64–65
  game:
    design, 53–55
    tester, 55
  graphic:
    artist, 52
    designer, 52
  illustration, 67–69
  script writers, 53
  signage, 57–58, 66–67
  storyboard artists, 53
Industry requirements, 36–38
Information interview, 120–121
Interior designer, 10, 92, 100–102, 107–108
Internet communications, 7
  web page design, 8–10, 72–75, 84–85
Interning, 111–127
  conferences, 121–123
  cooperative education, 116
  guidelines, 115–116
  information interview, 120–121
  portfolio, 118–120, 125–126

résumé, 117–118
trade shows, 121–123
Inverse kinematics (IK), 19

J

J.J. Sedelmaier Productions, Inc., 140
Jewelry design, 14–15, 92–94, 104–105
Jim Kesshem Productions, 63–64
Journals, 162

L

Lesh, David, 154

M

Magazines, 162
on-line, 8
Mendenhall, Cheryl, 62
[Metal] Studio, 139
Miami-Dade Community College Film and Video, 48
Mosaic, 20–21
Mouse, 21–22
Multimedia, 72, 80–82, 88

O

On-line magazines, 8

P

Package design, 72, 78–80, 86–87
Paraham Santana, Inc., 140
Photography, 13–14
commercial, 10, 72, 75–77
digital, 7, 75–77
food, 85–86
stock, 86

Portfolio, 118–120, 125–126
Poser 4.0, 19
Product:
designers, 91–109
display artist, 92
exhibit, 92, 97–100, 106–107
interior, 92, 100–102, 107–108
jewelry, 92–94, 104–105
toy, 92, 94–97, 105–106
evangelist, 28–29
Professional organizations, 163–164

R

Raritan Valley Community College Fine and Performing Arts, 48
Regional Occupation Programs, 34
Resources, 161–164
Résumé, 117–118

S

Salaries, 138–139
Santa Monica College, 40–42
School of Advertising Art, 44
Script writers, 53
Sculpting, 20
Signage, 42–43, 57–58, 66–67
Smith, Geoffrey, 154
Souders, Linda, 154, 157–158
Specialized training, 6
Springfield College Art Department, 48–49
Steve Morris Design, 140

Stock photography, 86
Storyboard artists, 53

T

Techno animations, 22–24
3-D, 20
3-D Central, 83
3-D Environments, 102
3-D Maker, 11
3-dd Digital Design, 83
Toy designer, 92, 94–97, 105–106
Trade shows, 121–123
Training, 33–49
advertising, 44
art institutes, 47
bachelor's degree, 35
cooperative, 116
creativity, 44–45
industry requirements, 36–38
Regional Occupation Programs, 34
sign painting, 42–43
specialized, 6
See also: specific schools and programs

V

Valencia Community College, Department of Graphics Technology, 49
Via, 140

W

Web page design, 8–10, 72–75, 84–85
Williams, Theo Stephan, 154
Writers, script, 53
WYSIWYG, 20–21